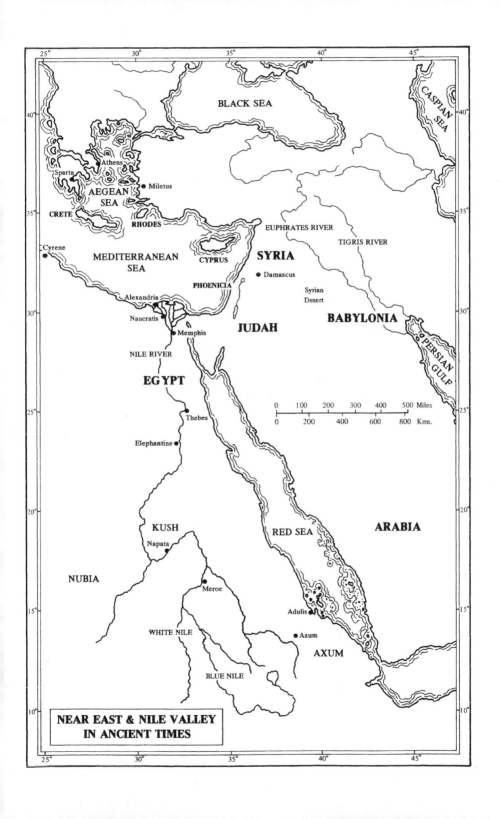

NEAR EAST & NILE VALLEY
IN ANCIENT TIMES

William Leo Hansberry

# AFRICA & AFRICANS

## AS SEEN BY CLASSICAL WRITERS

# William Leo Hansberry

AFRICAN HISTORY NOTEBOOK                    VOLUME II

# AFRICA & AFRICANS

## AS SEEN BY CLASSICAL WRITERS

Edited by Joseph E. Harris

Black Classic Press
Baltimore

Africa and Africans as Seen by Classical Writers

Published by Black Classic Press 2019

Library of Congress Control Number: 2018952989
Print book ISBN: 978-157478-154-0
E-book ISBN: 978-1-57478-160-1

Printed by BCP Digital Printing (www.bcpdigital.com)
an affiliate company of Black Classic Press Inc.
For a virtual tour of our publishing and printing facility visit:
https://www.c-span.org/video/?441322-2/tour-black-classic-press

Purchase Black Classic Press books from your favorite book seller
or order online at: www.blackclassicbooks.com

To request a list of titles, write:
Black Classic Press
P.O. Box 13414
Baltimore, MD 21203

*To the memory of*
*William Leo Hansberry and to his wife,*
*Myrtle Kelso Hansberry*

# William Leo Hansberry
# Pioneering Africanist
## A Note to the Black Classic Press Edition

The legacy of pioneering Africanist William Leo Hansberry (1894–1965) lives on today throughout the African Diaspora. As these volumes were prepared for republication, I recalled how I first became involved in part of that legacy. While preparing for my qualifying examinations at Northwestern University in 1958, I accepted a temporary position in the Department of History at Howard University, where I had received both my BA and MA degrees. Howard University did not offer a Ph.D. in history at that time, so Professor Rayford W. Logan recommended that I apply to Northwestern University for doctoral studies in its African Studies Program. Northwestern, along with Howard and Boston Universities, had been funded in 1954 as major centers for the study of Africa.

At Northwestern, I studied under a number of distinguished scholars in African studies: Professor Melville Herskovits, anthropologist at Northwestern; visiting historians Kenneth Dike from Nigeria, John Fage from England and Jan Vancina from Belgium, at the University of Wisconsin; and the political scientist Thomas Hodgkin from England. Because of my commitment to Howard University and the emergence of the African Studies Program there, I encouraged Professor Dike to visit Howard and contact Professor Hansberry. Dike readily accepted that idea, partly because he was interested in Howard University's reputation in African studies, and also because he knew that Hansberry had taught Nigeria's first President, Nnamdi Azikiwe. Dike was impressed by the size, extent and diversity of Hansberry's archives and promised to remain available for consultation regarding publication of Hansberry's works. However, I never knew what resulted from that relationship.

Africa was just beginning to emerge as a major research field, although Hansberry had been teaching the subject at Howard since the 1920s. Between 1958 and 1959, I was fortunate to share an office with Hansberry at Howard.

In addition to his teaching, Hansberry secured funds for African student scholarships, organized seminars and exhibits on Africa, and engaged in discussions that led to the founding of the African American Institute, which sponsored Africa House as a meeting place for African students. Hansberry also gave lectures at book club meetings, church gatherings, and other social events. These and other activities established his reputation as an Africanist and led to his national and international recognition, including the establishment of The Hansberry Institute of African Studies at the University of Nigeria in 1961 and his receiving the first African research award from the Haile Selassie I Prize Trust in 1964.

Hansberry was also an activist, who participated in the Fourth Pan-African Conference in 1927 in New York, joined students and faculty in 1934 in organizing the Ethiopian Research Council that lobbied for Ethiopia during the Italo-Ethiopian War, and encouraged some of his students to participate in post-war development in Ethiopia. Indeed, his pan-African writings, teaching, and service contributed significantly to sustaining intellectual, social, and political links between African Americans and Africans.

Thus, The William Leo Hansberry African History Notebook, two volumes: Pillars in Ethiopian History, and Africa and Africans As Seen by Classical Writers (published by Howard University Press in 1974 and 1977 respectively), found a ready and steady market among scholars, Africanists generally, and others. That demand, and the quality of Hansberry's work as a historian and pioneering Africanist, motivated Black Classic Press to republish both of those volumes since Howard University Press has ceased publishing.

The release of these volumes occurs at a time when the African Diaspora has become an established concept in a number of university programs, the media, and throughout the wider public. Although Hansberry did not frame his work as Diasporic, his 1935 proposal that Howard University establish a "Varia Africana" program presaged contemporary Africana programs, and his concept of pan-Africanism contributed to the continuity of the Diaspora tradition. It is in that context that Hansberry deserves recognition as a forerunner of global African Diaspora and pan African studies.

Joseph E. Harris,
Distinguished Professor Emeritus
Howard University
January 15, 2019

# Preface

This book represents decades of tedious research by the late Professor William Leo Hansberry. It was tedious not only because the many sources in several different languages had to be examined in translation but also because references to Africa in most of the classical works are few and far between, and are frequently bewildering even when located. To identify and comprehend better the classical references, Professor Hansberry also became a student and teacher of Greek and Roman history. After identifying the relevant sources, however, there remained the problem of physically locating them, because few libraries housed such old and little-used books. Consequently, Hansberry had to visit several of the major libraries in the world to complete his research for this and other subjects. In connection with this particular study, he not only conducted research at the principal libraries in the United States, but also spent considerable time at the British Museum, the Bodleian and Ashmolean at Oxford, the F. L. Griffith Library at Boars' Hill in England, the Bibliothèque Nationale in Paris, and archives in Ethiopia, Egypt, and the Sudan.

The determination and commitment of this pioneer Africanist can be more fully appreciated by recalling that most of his research was conducted between 1916 and 1954, a 38-year period when African studies had virtually no academic status in the United States and little support among philanthropists. Consequently, Professor Hansberry had to rely primarily on his own funds to finance his research and to purchase audiovisual aids for his research and classes. In spite of these difficulties, he was able to inaugurate the African Civilization Section of the History Department at Howard University in 1922. By 1924, it had enrolled over 800 students in three different courses and was the vanguard of African studies in this country.

In 1925 Hansberry sponsored at Howard University a symposium, "The Cultures and Civilizations of Negro Peoples in Africa," at which twenty-eight scholarly papers were presented by some of his students from the United States, Panama, Guyana, and Columbia. The topics discussed by the panelists reflected the intellectual currents of pan-Africanism for which Howard University has stood since Hansberry's efforts.

The 1920s were indeed the seedtime of African studies at Howard University, and although he received little financial or spiritual encouragement from his colleagues and the university administration during those years, the ambitious and determined Hansberry set high goals for African studies at that institution. He wrote,

> No institution is more obligated and no Negro school is in a
> better position to develop such a program than Howard. No
> institution has access to specialized libraries—the Moorland
> Collection [at Howard], and city repositories; nowhere else are
> the thought and planning put forth; no better courses exist
> anywhere else; there are no better trained students anywhere, by
> virtue of racial background. This is the area in which Howard
> has the most promising and immediate opportunity to distinguish
> itself as a leader in the general cause of public enlightenment.*

Hansberry obviously perceived Howard University as the

*HPP (Hansberry's Private Papers), and quoted in Harris, *Pillars in Ethiopian History*, pp. 10,11.

X

emerging leader of African studies in the United States, and to help secure that goal he proposed several projects and planned the puublication of source books designed for school use. He hoped these would arouse "Negro peoples in particular to make a specific effort to revive and develop to the full those creative and spiritual powers which . . . are Nature's preeminent gifts to the African."†

Hansberry not only believed that blacks should commit themselves more fully to the writing of their own history, but that they should pursue a pan-Africanist approach by virtue of the common origin and historical experiences of the African "at home and abroad," He further believed that academicians should made their knowledge available ay all levels of society. In his own case, he lectured widely in the United States and Africa to specialists and laymen; he wrote for a variety of journals; he helped to organize the Ethiopian Research Council in 1934 and the African-American Institute in 1952 to stimulate interest in African affairs; he testified before the Senate Committee on Foreign Affairs on behalf of aid to Africa; he recruited teachers and technicians for Ethiopia; and above all he untiringly gave his counsel to students, especially African students who, in his judgment, needed an Afro-centric perspective on their heritage.

The apogee of Hansberry's professional career came during the 1960s, when he was awarded honorary degrees by Virginia State College, Morgan State College, and the University of Niageria at Nsukka. The latter institution also established the Hansberry Institute of African Studies, where Hansberry served as Distinguished Visiting Professor in 1963. In 1964 he became the first recipient of the African research award from the Haile Selassie I Prize Trust.

Professor Hansberry was indeed a pioneer Africanist

†Ibid., p. 12

whose life deserves a fuller study.* As Professor Williston H. Lofton, Hansberry's friend and colleague at Howard University, has written,

> Along with W.E.B. DuBois and Carter G. Woodson, Hansberry probably did more than any other scholar in these early days to advance the study of the culture and civilization of Africa.

This volume, like the first one, is intended primarily for the general reader, but the Africanist, especially the historian, should benefit from both the content and interpretations of the African references by the classical writers whose works are examined. To date, the best comprehensive and authoritative book in this general field is Frank Snowden's *Blacks in Antiquity: Ethiopians in the Greco-Roman Experience* (Cambridge, Mass., 1970). Snowden and Hansberry were longtime friends and colleagues at Howard University and probably discussed their common interests. Snowden's book is more technical and more concerned about Africans in the Greco-Roman world; it places considerable emphasis on artistic representation of blacks in antiquity. This volume by Hansberry is concerned principally with classical writers' comments about Africans below the northern region, and stresses geographical and historical notices. The two books are complementary.

As in volume one, I gratefully acknowledge the valuable cooperation and assistance of Myrtle Kelso Hansberry, Profes-

---

*For a fuller biographical account, see "William Leo Hansberry: Profile of a Pioneer Africanist," in Joseph E. Harris, ed., *Pillars in Ethiopian History: The William Leo Hansberry African History Notebook* (vol. 1, 1974). The following articles are also helpful: Nnamdi Azikiwe, "Eulogy on William Leo Hansberry," *Negro History Bulletin* 28 (December 1965); Williston H. Lofton, "William Leo Hansberry: The Man and His Mission," *Freedomways*, vol. 6, no. 2 (1966); Raymond J. Smyke, "William Leo Hansberry: Tribute to a Heretic," *Africa Report* (November 1965) and "Pioneer Africanist," *West Africa* (November 20, 1965); James Spady, "Dr. William Leo Hansberry: The Legacy of an African Hunter," *A Current Bibliography on African Affairs*, vol. 3, no. 10 (November-December 1970); and *A Tribute to the Memory of Professor William Leo Hansberry* (Department of History, Howard, 1972).

sor Hansberry's widow, without whose untiring efforts over the years these papers would not have been published. I again thank Charles F. Harris who, when I first undertook the editorship of these materials, was a senior editor at Random House and is now executive director of Howard University Press. I am also grateful to Professor Ephraim Isaac at Harvard University for reading the chapter, "Ancient Designations for Ethiopia." My gratitude is also extended to the Stetson Library staff of Williams College for their kind assistance.

I am sure that had Professor Hansberry lived to publish this volume, it would have been quite different. I could not, as I believe no one could, hope to duplicate his own plans for all of these notes and comments that appear throughout his papers spanning fifty years. (One set of notes on which this study is based was dated 1931.) In spite of this difficulty and the several years that have elapsed since Hansberry began seriously to synthesize his materials, I believe this volume will make a creditable contribution to the general field of African history, especially the ancient period.

Except for a few editorial modifications and some reorganization, the following chapters are largely Professor Hansberry's work and reflect his style. This not only justifies the title as his notebook; it also facilitates a more accurate evaluation of his ideas and research.

The above was written while I was a professor of history at Williams College and before I joined the faculty at Howard University in 1975. I now am even more convinced that Professor Hansberry's influence as a teaching historian and humanist can never be fully determined. During my travels to Africa and the Caribbean over the past few years, I have encountered several persons in various professions who recalled Leo Hansberry as the Howard University professor who really provided the inspiration and perspective they needed to succeed as black persons.

Professor Hansberry's career as a historian also demonstrates that scholarly impact does not necessarily correlate with actual publications. His influence far surpasses that which could have emanated from his several published articles, and a key reason for this is that he stood virtually alone in teaching the content and methodology needed for the historical reconstruction of Africa's past. His files and the testimony of many of his students reveal the meticulous efforts he took to demonstrate the usefulness to African research of the anthropological, geographical, archeological, and linguistic methods. His classes were well attended and his lectures were notable for methodological discussions and fresh interpretations of old data. Hansberry's students, therefore, partook of a quality apprenticeship in studying African history at Howard University.

The spirit of Hansberry mingled among those proponents of the African-centered perspective on Black history, and several of the leaders of the Black studies movement of the 1960s and 1970s were his protégés. Future generations now have access to another segment of his works in this second volume of his *Notebook,* which further illustrates the scope, depth, and continued relevance of the research and insight of this pioneer historian.

Joseph E. Harris
Department of History
Howard University
1977

# Contents

# Editor's Introduction

This volume reveals Professor Hansberry's familiarity with a wide range of sources and data in ancient African history. Since Hansberry's study is not primarily a narrative, my introduction will provide a concise historical context within which the subsequent chapters may be understood.

By the sixth century B.C. the Greeks had established a settlement in Naukratis, Egypt, and were in a good position to interact with blacks from Africa. That Greek awareness of Ethiopia (the African territory south of Egypt) was considerable from that time on is attested to by contemporary literature. The first indication of that awareness in classical literature appears in Homer's *Iliad* and *Odyssey*. Then followed references scattered in the works of Aeschylus, Sophocles, Euripides, Hesiod, Herodotus, and others. Since contacts between the Greeks and Africans no doubt existed for centuries before that, the literature does not reflect a particular consciousness of black people until around the sixth century B.C. The reason for this is very likely related to the political consciousness of the Greeks. Aeschylus, Sophocles, and Euripides, for example, were Athenians; and although their Greek friend Herodotus, was not Athenian, he and they witnessed the rise of Athenian democracy and naval power and understood the relationship of those developments to the evolving national pride of the Greeks, especially following the wars with Persia in 500–449 B.C. This greater political awareness concerning all surrounding peoples, which of course included Africans, was clearly reflected in the writings of the poets and playwrights.

At the same time, the writing of prose became a notable feature of Greek literature, especially in history, philosophy, and the natural sciences. Although Hecataeus is sometimes referred to as the real founder of the study of history and geography, the distinction, "Father of History," is more generally given to Herodotus for his serious efforts to recount the past from oral traditions and the scanty written sources, including works by Hecataeus. The growing popularity of prose writing also may be attributed to the rising political consciousness of the Greeks. A people aware that they were active participants in the drama of history were indeed encouraged to examine their own past and that of others. This interest led to extensive travels in Africa by ancient Greek writers of history and geography: Herodotus went as far south as Elephantine (Aswan); Agatharchides lived in Alexandria; Diodorus spent considerable time in several parts of Egypt; and Strabo traveled up the Nile to Syene. Thus, the inquisitive and literary example of Herodotus and others provided valuable data on geography, trade, local customs, wars, and international relations, and also established a tradition of writing professional history. That Herodotus and others of his era were sometimes fascinated by the extravagant, and, by modern standards, lacked a sophisticated methodology and systematically critical and analytic approach is understandable; they, however, were pioneers and the critical use of their works can provide valuable insights into ancient African and, indeed, world history, as Hansberry shows in these essays.

The Greek literary tradition, drawing upon reports of

travelers, merchants, and soldiers, enhanced Greek knowledge of the people, regions, and products of inner Africa (Ethiopia). Napata became a major focus of Greek attention, and for understandable reasons. It was the seat of power for Kush, the first state known to us south of Egypt, and was led by Piankhy in its conquest of Egypt during the eighth century. Kush retained control over the northern state until 654 B.C., when the Assyrians forced a successor, Tanwetamani, to retreat southward. Subsequently, around 591 B.C., the seat of government was shifted to Meroe, which enjoyed a greater rainfall and thus a greater and more reliable supply of food. There was also a richer pastureland, available iron ore and timber for smelting, and a strategic location for trade along the Nile River, the Red Sea, and the western Sudan. Meroe was able to flourish for nearly a thousand years, from the sixth century B.C. until approximately 350 A.D.

The conquest of Egypt by Alexander the Great in 332 B.C. introduced a new chapter in Greco-African relations. The Ptolemies developed new trade routes into the African hinterland, and commercial stations appeared in several areas along the Nile. When the Ptolemaic dynasty was defeated in 30 B.C. and Egypt annexed to the Roman Empire, the Romans continued the advance into the south and the establishment of direct contacts with societies in that area. In the course of those activities and the accompanying wars, the Romans were able to produce firsthand accounts of inner Africa and its peoples. Preeminent among these accounts were those of Pliny the Elder.

The early Greeks and Romans described all the black people inhabiting the lands south of the Mediterranean coast of Africa as Ethiopians, and that is the sense in which the term is used in this book unless otherwise indicated. That the Greeks and Romans were highly conscious of the blackness and physical type of the Ethiopian is amply documented. The crucial question is what that sensitivity reflected. Many writers on this subject have concluded that no denigratory racial attitudes and concepts should be attributed to the ancients. In evidence, they cite classical references to Ethiopians as "pious and just" and "blameless," and point to the general absence of derogatory treatment. Some of the evidence supports this line of reason. There is, however, another stream of records which did characterize Ethiopians as "mysterious" people with "tightly curled or wooly hair; broad and flattened noses; lips thick, often puffy and everted; and prognathous"—characterizations not complimentary in those societies. In addition, Herodotus spoke of Africans as having "speech [that] resembles the shrieking of a Bat rather than the Language of Men"; and Pliny the Elder spoke of those who "by report have no heads but mouth and eies in their breasts." There are other similar examples. Moreover, while it may be argued, as some writers have, that the proverb "to wash an Ethiopian white" meant no more than to emphasize that something made by nature or God cannot be changed, it is difficult to resist the argument that consciously or not, the statement contained seeds of racial denigration. The main point here is to remind the reader that there were two streams of information emanating from the classical writers and that the unfavorable characterization has had the greatest influence on the image and treatment of blacks in our own times.

It was that latter characterization which motivated Professor Hansberry to persist in the study of ancient views of Africans, to correct the record and to reveal the true picture as far as that was possible. Hansberry fully understood the social tragedy of the heritage in which Africans were not only denigrated but were taught to despise themselves and neglect the study of their history. In this context he recognized the historical links between the "African at home and abroad," an expression he employed on several occasions. He thus pursued a pan-African tradition.* He believed that African peoples themselves had to become more responsible for the reconstruction of their history. Through his own research, he sought to correct old myths and stereotypes and to shed light on that positive stream of information left by the ancient writers. His purpose was neither to deny the tradition of denigration nor to glorify the black heritage, for as he noted, "The African, like the rest of mankind, has nothing to gain in the long run by suppressing the truth and suggesting the false for chauvinistic reasons."

Two final points deserve note. First, few scholars have seriously appreciated the relationship between traditional documentary evidence and art, the plastic arts in particular.** Professor Hansberry recognized this important relationship many years ago, as his methodology and comments in this study confirm. The portrayal of Africans in ancient art was frequent and very likely based on direct evidence.

The second point is related to the first as well as to the general statements in this introduction. Many non-Africans in the Mediterranean world during ancient and subsequent times were exposed in one way or another to Africans and their achievements. Not only did Africans develop a significant commercial influence in the Mediterranean area and Asia, they also established a distinguished military record in their local conquests as well as in the armies of the Greeks and Romans. African soldiers also attacked and resisted Greek

*For a discussion of Hansberry's broader pan-African activities see *Pillars in Ethiopian History: The William Leo Hansberry African History Notebook*, vol. 1, chapter 1.

**Two scholars who have are: Grace H. Beardsley, *The Negro in Greek and Roman Civilization: A Study of the Ethiopian Type* (New York, 1929; reissued, 1967); Frank Snowden, *Blacks in Antiquity: Ethiopians in the Greco-Roman Experience* (Cambridge, Mass., 1970), and Snowden, "Ethiopians and the Graeco-Roman World," *The African Diaspora: Interpretive Essays* (Harvard University Press, 1976), Martin L. Kilson and Robert I. Rotberg, editors.

and Roman invaders. In short, in addition to trade and to Greek and Roman settlements in Naukratis and elsewhere in North Africa, which afforded opportunities for direct knowledge about indigenous societies, the political and military power of Africans in Egypt, Napata, and Meroe, and the African presence abroad all contributed to the image non-Africans had of the continent and its people. The extent to which racism, colonialism, and imperialism distorted that image is a much more familiar story which is beyond the principal concern of this study.

One critic, W. Robert Connor, boldly states that Homer's "selection of a black-skinned and wooley-haired herald for Odysseus, Eurybates, is part of the respectful consciousness of black power on the edge of the Greek world."* More correctly, that "black power" was the outer edge of a dynamic and innovative Africa, whose contributions to world civilization have yet to be fully appreciated.

*Cited in: Kilson and Rotberg, *The African Diaspora,* p. 20.

# Africa and Africans
*As Seen by Classical Writers*

# I

# Ancient Designations for Ethiopia

## GREEK DESIGNATIONS

The earliest use of the word Ethiopia, as far as present records reveal, is found in the *Iliad* and the *Odyssey* of Homer, dating from the ninth century B.C.; henceforth, it was a very familiar expression in classical literature. Among the post-Homeric famous poems and dramas in which references to Ethiopia or the Ethiopians occur, to mention only a few, are Hesiod's *Theogony* and *Works and Days*, Aeschylus' *Prometheus Bound*, Apollonius' *Argonautica*, Quintus' *Posthomerica*, Virgil's *Aeneid* and the *Ethiopis* of Arctinus of Miletus. In the field of prose, both terms are repeatedly mentioned by the historians, Herodotus, Diodorus, Josephus, and Dion Cassius; by the geographers, Hecataeus, Ephorus, Eratosthenes, Agatharchides, and Strabo; by the naturalist Pliny; and by the romancers, Callisthenes and Heliodorus.

Theories concerning the etymology of the term Ethiopia vary somewhat among different writers. Pliny stated that it was derived from Aethiops, son of Vulcan, the god of metalworking and of fire, and who was, it may be pointed out, a kind of Greek counterpart of the Ethiopian god Bes. Other writers have pointed out that *Aethiops*, meaning "the Glowing" or "the Black," was a surname of Zeus, under which this god was worshipped in the island of Chios. The scholarly consensus, however, is that the term was derived ultimately from

the Greek word meaning approximately, "A man with a (sun)
burned or black face." Although the *Iliad* and the *Odyssey* contain the earliest known use of the word Ethiopia, it is hardly
likely, to quote Sir E. A. Budge, "that Homer invented the
name Ethiopia or Ethiopians." We may assume, said this distinguished antiquarian, "that both terms were well known ap-
pellations and were already in existence" when the *Iliad* and
the *Odyssey* were being crystallized into definite form. It may
be pointed out in passing that this view finds considerable
support in archeological discoveries, in that Ethiopians were
known to have been domiciled in and otherwise in contact
with the Aegean area hundreds of years before Homer's time.

The territory included by the Greeks under the designation Ethiopia varies somewhat from age to age. Writers of the
earlier period, particularly those composing the epic cycle, applied Ethiopia and Ethiopians to lands and peoples in both
Africa and Asia; the latter continent was included apparently
with good cause, for more recent discoveries and research
have established that in ancient times a blackskinned people,
or Aethiops, constituted an important part of the populations
of Arabia, Mesopotamia, Persia, and India. Homer alluded to
the Ethiopians of the two continents, noting that one division
was situated towards the sunrise and another towards the sunset; for the Ethiopians are, says the poet:

> *A race divided, whom the sloping rays*
> *The rising and the setting sun surveys.*

Herodotus referred to eastern Ethiopians and western
Ethiopians in connection with the polyglot army of Xerxes;
and Strabo wrote that "ancient Greeks ... designated the
whole of southern countries towards the ocean ... on the
coasts of both Asia and Africa, as Ethiopia." He specifically cited the ancient geographer Ephorus, whose works are now

lost, as holding this opinion and further said that "if the moderns have confined the appellation Ethiopians to refer only to peoples who dwell above [south of] Egypt, this must not be allowed to interfere with the meaning of the ancients." In the later periods, especially during the closing phases of the classical age, the Asian Ethiopians disappeared gradually from remembrance, and the regions concerned took on other and more distinctive names. The Ethiopians of Africa, however, by virtue of the greater permanency of their civilization and through their more intimate contact with Greece by way of Ptolemaic and Roman Egypt, came more frequently into view. Thus the term Ethiopia in the writings of the later classical authors came to refer almost exclusively to the African region to the south of Egypt.

The boundaries of the African lands designated by the Greek geographers as Ethiopia were for the most part rather indefinite, but roughly speaking, the regions thus named corresponded in a general way to the territory known at the present time as the Republic of the Sudan. Over some three or four hundred years it became customary to speak of northeastern Africa south of Egypt as part of the "Kingdom of Ethiopia." This practice has been called "a literary usurpation and an historical error," and there is something to be said for this point of view. For it is true that although Ethiopia was sometimes used as a general designation for the whole of eastern Africa south of Egypt, the prevailing practice was to restrict the term in the main to the territory lying further to the north and northwest, or what, as just stated, corresponds roughly to the Republic of the Sudan. Hence, the designation Ethiopia in this work generally refers to the last-named area; and when the occasion requires the use of the term in the larger or broader Greek sense, this will be indicated by the designation Greater Ethiopia.

Since the name Ethiopia seems to have been a distinctively European or Greek product and therefore a relatively late creation so far as Nilotic history is concerned, it need hardly be urged that the term had little if any currency among the peoples native to the area. Indeed, so far as we know, the ancient Ethiopians, as odd as it may seem, never called themselves "Ethiopians" or their land "Ethiopia," nor did the ancient Egyptians or the adjacent Asian nations, seemingly, ever make use of these terms in referring to their "dusky" neighbors and contemporaries. It is only by reason of the popularity of classical literature in the modern scheme of thought that the name Ethiopia has come to have the currency it does at the present day. In discussing the early history of the country, particularly its own internal relations and its relations with its Oriental neighbors, it will be necessary at times to press into service certain designations employed in these several communities. A brief review of these will now follow.

## ETHIOPIAN DESIGNATIONS

B ecause of the relatively recent discovery of the more important Ethiopian records that are now available to us, together with the difficulties that still attend the efforts of philologists to make translations of them, history is not yet very familiar with or very certain of the names by which the Ethiopians designated their country or themselves. Notwithstanding these limitations, a considerable degree of progress has been made in this direction. Particularly notable are the works of Dr. A. H. Sayce and Mr. G. L. Griffith of Oxford University. Through the studies by these two distinguished scholars, a most valuable inscription discovered in Ethiopia in 1914 made it reasonably certain that the Ethiopians designated their country, or at least a goodly part of it, as the land of Qevs (Kesh). The discovery and transliteration of these inscriptions marked a very important advance in the study of Nilotic and Oriental history, for according to the authorities named, the Ethiopian word Qevs (or Kesh) may be identified with the Egyptian word Kush and the Hebrew word Cush, the designations which were generally applied to Ethiopia for thousands of years by the Egyptians and the peoples of western Asia. In a similar way the appellation Kesht or Keshli is thought to be the Ethiopian equivalent of the Egyptian Kashto and the Hebrew Cushite, names which also had a widespread currency in the ancient world.

It was formerly thought that Kush or Cush and their derivations were of Egyptian or Hebrew origin, but the discovery of their counterparts in an Ethiopian record seem to indicate that the words were indigenous to the country and peoples to which they were generally applied. In addition to the more inclusive term Kesh, there are also available scores of designations by which the Ethiopians distinguished particular districts or sections of their country; but for our present purpose it is sufficient to mention only a few of these. According to E. A. Budge's translation and interpretation of the inscription on the stele of Nastasen, belonging to a king who lived about the fourth century B.C., the northern part of the country, corresponding roughly to what is known at the present time as Nubia, bore the name of Kenset, while the general region to the south as far as the juncture of the Blue and the White Niles seems to have been designated as the "land of Alu." The great stele of Amonrenas, dating about four hundred years later, gives, according to Dr. Sayce's rendering of the text, the designation "land of Athi (ye)" to an important division of the northern country, while the regions to the south are known as the "land of Yesbe." Whether the variations in names recorded on the two steles represent actual changes that had come about in the intervening period or whether they are the results of difficulties attending attempts at transliteration of Ethiopian text is not certain.

The Ethiopian inscriptions that are now available contain the names of a hundred or more towns and cities which were located within the country and in neighboring regions, but little if any advantage would be gained by listing them at this point. It may be of interest, however, to note that the great and ancient metropolis and chief capital of the country, the celebrated city of Meroe, so often mentioned in the writings of classical authors, was designated by the Ethiopians themselves as Me-rh-e-u; and of equal interest is the discovery that Armi was the Ethiopian name for the great city of Rome. The ancient Ethiopians appear to have had designations which covered wide stretches of land with diverse groups of people, an indication of united consciousness, a prerequisite for nationalism.

## EGYPTIAN DESIGNATIONS

The ancient Egyptians knew Ethiopia and its people under a variety of names. The earliest mention of the country, so far as present records go, is contained in an inscription on what is known as the Palermo Stone* and dates from the early part of the third millennium B.C. Here the region immediately south of Egypt is designated "the land of the Nehsyuw" ("Nehsyw" or "Nehesi"), according to the transliterations of different Egyptologists. In the opinion of many scholars the word Nehsyuw meant, in Egyptian, "black"; hence the "land of Nehsyuw" was the Egyptian equivalent of the "land of the blacks." During the same period, the Egyptians also referred to this region as *Khent* ("the

*The Palermo stone is the earliest remaining record of year lists which serve in establishing Egyptian chronology. *Ed.*

borderland") and as Ta-Sti, ("land of the bow"), and the people were called the Steu or "bowmen." Budge thinks that the northern section of Ethiopia was also anciently designated, as at present, by a form of the word Nubia, being derived from the Egyptian word nub, meaning "gold"; hence, in his opinion, the district bore a designation equivalent to the "land of gold."

In the second millennium B.C., following hard on waves of northward migrations and a series of attacks upon Egypt by Ethiopians out of the southern regions, the word Kush as a designation of Ethiopia made its appearance in Egyptian records and continued to be the chief name applied to the lands of the south until the collapse of Egyptian civilization. During the period of the New Empire, which saw Egypt's development into the greatest cultural and political power of the early ancient world, the term Kush became one of the most widely used and familiar expressions in Egyptian geographical and historical literature. The exact boundaries of the territory included by the Egyptians under this famous term are not very clear; in the opinion of some scholars, the appellation was applied chiefly to the northern part of the country, while others think that it was used as a designation for the southern lands as far south as the Blue Nile. Although this celebrated term was formerly thought to be of Egyptian or perhaps Hebrew origin, the recent discovery of the equivalent Qevs (Kesh) in Ethiopian inscriptions points to the possibility of a southern or Ethiopian derivation. Almost as common in Egyptian literature were the terms Punt and Ta Ta-Neter, applied by the Egyptians to that part of Greater Ethiopia extending roughly from the headwaters of the Atbara and the Blue Nile eastward to the Indian Ocean, the Arabian Gulf, and the southern reaches of the Red Sea.

With the exception of Kush, no ancient land figured more prominently in the historical and religious writings of the ancient Egyptians than did the often-mentioned region of Punt. Many a pharoah records with pride the success of great trading expeditions sent thither, and indeed the historical and religious lore of Egypt throughout its long history celebrated the territory as a kind of holy land because it was considered to be the birthplace of the Egyptian race and the original homeland of many of the great Egyptian gods.

In addition to the foregoing designations used by the Egyptians to distinguish the larger territorial divisions of Greater Ethiopia, mention may also be made of the fact that the historical literature of Egypt abounds in lists of Ethiopian towns and cities and names that were applied to smaller or localized districts, a circumstance which incidentally reflects the extent of Egyptian knowledge concerning the minor political or geographical divisions and the urban centers of the country. One document alone, the *Inscription of Una*, dating from the early part of the third millennium B.C., records the names of six districts in northern Ethiopia; and on the wall of a pylon in Thebes, built about 1500 B.C., there are inscribed the names of 242 towns, cities, and districts located in Ethiopia and Punt. It is clear that Ethiopia was well known to the Egyptian scribes and analysts even in the early periods of ancient history.

## ASIAN DESIGNATIONS

A word or two about certain Asian designations of Egypt's southern neighbor will bring this section to a close. The records of antiquity show that, in the course of their long history, Ethiopia and her peoples were often in contact particularly with some of the ancient nations and peoples of the Near East. Traditions preserved in the poems of the epic cycle, through the Memnon legend, connected the royal house of Ethiopia with the royal house of Persia and Homeric Troy; the annals of Assyrian and Babylonian kings contain several references to relations with their Ethiopian contemporaries, and some of the most interesting and stirring passages in the ancient writings of the Hebrews center on events and episodes in which the land and peoples styled by the Greeks as Ethiopia and Ethiopians are frequently and prominently mentioned. The older Asian nations, however, never made use of the Greek terminology in recording their relationships with their African contemporaries.

In the Talmud and in the Old Testament there repeatedly occurs a series of geographical, historical, and ethnological expressions which are traditionally considered to have been generally used over a large part of western and southwestern Asia in referring to Ethiopia and to Ethiopian peoples. The most familiar of these is the term Cush and expressions derived from it, such as Cushan, Cushanreshathaim, Cushi, Cushite, and the Cushites. Unfortunately, however, the exact meaning of some of the passages in which these expressions occur is not always clear, and scholars of rabbinical and Biblical literature are often at odds over their interpretation. The confusion arises from the use of the term Cush and words based on it to designate lands and peoples in both Asia and Africa; it occasionally happens that from the context of a passage, it cannot be told to just which continent the expression is intended to refer. But no matter how confusing a passage may be on this score, it is generally agreed among scholars that the designations, in whatever form they may appear, are traditionally or historically connected with some "dusky-hued" or "black-skinned" people. For example, Cush, the son of Ham, mentioned in the genealogical scheme given in the tenth chapter of Genesis, has been customarily treated as a kind of traditional or eponymous ancestor of black people. In the authorized version of the Old Testament, the term Cush, when referring to a land or country, has been translated, except in Genesis, as Ethiopia; and again, in rabbinical literature, the terms Cushite, the Cushites, and the like are generally understood to mean Negroid. Hence the designation Cush and the other specified forms of the word, whether applying to localities or peoples in Africa or Asia, seem to reflect etymological, ethnological, and historical complexes whose roots go back ultimately to Ethiopia.

It has been mentioned that it was formerly thought that the term Cush might possibly have been of Egyptian or Hebrew origin, but the recent discovery of its equivalent Qevs (or Kesh) in Ethiopian records seems to indicate, as we have previously suggested, an inner African or Ethiopian beginning. Just why the term was used as a designation of Asian peoples (it was applied to peoples in both Arabia and Mesopotamia) is not clear. It is another one of those many puzzling historical and ethnological problems connected with the complex and little-understood history of the ancient Near East. It may be suggested, however, that it may reflect invasions and migrations out of Ethiopia into Asia, such as are known to have taken place in Africa in the third and second millenniums B.C., when the Ethiopians pushed their way northward along the Nile Valley in Nubia and into Upper Egypt.

In the Assyrian inscriptions recording the fearful clashes which took place in the sixth century B.C. between the king of Ethiopia and the great monarchs of Assyria in their struggle for the hegemony of the civilized world, Ethiopia is again designated as Cush or Kush, and Meroe, the principal city of Ethiopia, is frequently metioned under the name of Mirukh. Here we doubtless have but another version of Qevs or Kesh and Me-rh-e-u, the names by which the Ethiopians themselves designated respectively their country and their capital.

In the Old Testament books of Genesis, Ezekiel, and Jeremiah, the designation Put as a geographical expression frequently appears. By some scholars this is thought to be the Hebrew name for the classical Libya, the country immediately west of Egypt; but by other scholars it is interpreted as applying to that part of greater Ethiopia styled by the Egyptians as Punt.

Clearly, the term Ethiopia and the geographical region south of Egypt were fairly well known during the classical era. It is this region to which most of the classical references to Africa apply.

# II

# A Preliminary Critique of Classical Sources

I n the beginnings of European literature, few names are better known and none is older than that of Ethiopia. Europe's earliest poetry sings of no foreign people quite so romantic; its geography records no country more distant; and its efforts at history memorializes no nation thought more ancient than that designated by this celebrated name. Homer, "Prince of Poets," the first in time among geographers, and, by some of the ancients, credited above Herodotus as the "Father of History," makes frequent use of the term in the *Iliad* and the *Odyssey*; and in post-Homeric times, several writers of similar bent followed the same course in many a classic theme of traditional renown. In this group most lovers of ancient literature will doubtless recall easily enough Hesiod's allusion in *Theogony* and in *Works and Days*, Aeschylus' passage in *Prometheus Bound*, Euripides' allusion in the fragment of the *Phaethon*, and the fate and fortune of Andromeda as told by Hyginus Apollodorus and Sophocles; but for similar references and allusions in the works of authors of lesser fame the memory is doubtless not so keen. To neglect Apollonius' *Argonautica*, Quintus' *Posthomerica*, and the fragments of the *Ethiopis* by Arctinus of Miletus would be indeed a grave oversight in such a survey; for these, no less than the more familiar creations, provide valuable clues for properly estimating the far-flung character of Ethiopia's name and fame in the circles of poetry and drama in the pre-classical period.

The classics abound in references and allusions to Ethiopia and the Ethiopians. Indeed, with the exception of Hellas and Hellas' own heroes, no land and no peoples are more persistently mentioned throughout the long and brilliant course of classical literature. It is a curious fact that centuries before the geographical and historical terms Babylon and Assyria, Persia, Carthage, and Etruria, or for that matter the terms Greece and Rome themselves, had made their first appearance in the writings of classical authors, Ethiopia was already an old and familiar expression; and long after the names Babylon, Assyria, Carthage, and Etruria had become scarcely more than vague memories, preserved only in the morgue of history, the hoary designation Ethiopia continued in use as the appellation of a nation which the later writers of classical antiquity regarded as contemporary with their own native lands. Homer and Hesiod, who lived in the dawn of European literature, frequently referred to the distant African territory and its "dusky" inhabitants, while not one of the ancient states just named is mentioned a single time. Again, the eventful years between the age of Pericles and the age of the earlier Caesars, when classical literature was at the peak of its development, Ethiopia and the Ethiopians were favorite and familiar topics with most of the leading poets, geographers, and historians. And finally, in the twilight of the classical age when the "glory that was Greece" and the "grandeur that was Rome" were capable of casting but a faint afterglow on the literary horizon, Heliodorus, Stephanus of Byzantium, and Olympadorus sought to enliven the fading literature of the dying world by giving Ethiopia a prominent place in the historical stories and romantic tales which they endeavored to tell. It is not necessary to stress that the historian who is bent upon making the story of the celebrated African state the burden of special study must become intimately acquainted with what the ancients of classical times had to say on this matter.

From the foregoing considerations two interesting observations may be made. The first is that the very earliest literate communities of Europe were evidently "Ethiopia conscious;" and the second is that the name Ethiopia and its derivatives are, as territorial and ethnic expressions, among the oldest living terms known to the geographical and historical literature of Europe.

An additional word about this second observation is perhaps necessary. As geographical and ethnographical expressions the terms Ethiopia and the Ethiopians are, as we have already said, frequently used by Homer in both the *Iliad* and the *Odyssey*, and the land and peoples to whom the poet-geographer on these occasions refers have continued to be thus designated to our own day. There are indeed but few names of nations and peoples that have seen longer and more continuous service in the science of geography, in the art of poetry, or in the science and art of history. With those who were pioneer laborers in these fields, Ethiopia was indeed an old and time-worn expression centuries before most of the more famous and familiar names now associated with antiquity had yet made their first appearance in European literature. When compared in this respect with Carthage, Greece, and Rome, or even Persia, Babylon, and Assyria, Ethiopia proves the greater patriarch by several hundred years. For it is a fact that in neither the *Iliad* nor the *Odyssey* nor the poems of Hesiod—the starting points of all western poetry, history, and geography—is there to be found a single reference to any one of these celebrated states or empires; and as territorial and ethnic expressions, all but two of them have long since been relegated to the morgue of history. On the score of age, the term Ethiopia indeed outranks even the hoary name Egypt itself, long and rightfully regarded as one of the very oldest and the very brightest stars recorded in the large lexicon of historical antiquity.

In the *Iliad*, the earlier of the Homeric sagas and the genesis of historical geography, Egypt (or Aegyptus) occurs but once, and then only as an auxiliary designation, that is to say, in connection with Thebes, "Egyptian Thebes." Ethiopia (or Aethiopia), however, is twice mentioned, stands alone, and is in its own right a proper name. In the *Odyssey* the honors are about evenly divided; but Hesiod, the first great poet after Homer, while referring twice to Ethiopia, nowhere mentions Egypt. And in this connection, it may be recalled that in the classical world a tradition was current that Egypt was the scion of Ethiopia.

Here, then, is foreshadowed our apology, if such should be required, for beginning this study of Ethiopia's history and civilization with certain preliminary observations on the position held by this ancient land in the beginnings of early European tradition. It became customary in the modern world to associate Ethiopia and Europe in much the same general way as dominant contemporary thought associates the expressions Negro and Nordic. More specifically, the popular conception is that the former signifies a land and people which are, and always have been, inferior to the land and people designated by the latter. The one was thought of mainly in the terms of savagery and slavery—as a country and a race that have only provided "hewers of wood and drawers of water" in the established social orders of history; the other was generally pictured, in the folk-mind at least, as an immemorial fount of culture where chivalry had its beginnings, and knighthood was always in flower. If relationships existed between the one land and the other, they must have been like that between Negro slave and Nordic master, or as of later years, like that between the colonial subject and the imperial governor. A casual survey of early European traditions regarding Ethiopia reveals, however, that such notions are ill-founded.

But what have ill-founded popular notions concerning the position of Ethiopia in early European tradition to do with a study of the history and civilization of the ancient land with which we are here mainly concerned? Two pertinent and legitimate reasons may be advanced. In the first place, an acquaintance with the real position of ancient Ethiopia in early European tradition will serve as a valuable corrective to the approbrious and mistaken connotations which were attached to the name Ethiopia and to peoples and things Ethiopian, connotations which certain historical and social developments caused to become almost universally accepted as genuine and original by the learned and the unlearned world of the present day. In other words, this introductory discussion has as its objective the rehabilitation of that attitude of mind which prevailed in the lands and among the peoples who originated the terms Ethiopia and Ethiopians as designations of a culture and people which they knew at first hand, or at any rate, better than medieval and modern literature has imagined. This is an effort to provide the readers with what seems to be the correct mental slant which they must take towards the ancient Ethiopians if they are to arrive at an approximation of the truth about the people and their land.

The second reason for this introductory effort is to call to the attention of the reader not already so informed, the fact that certain types of myths and legends, those of a more or less historical cast, are not necessarily always the creations of idle fancy but often have valuable grains of historical truth in them. An additional reason for stressing this fact here is to provide a general background for certain suggestions and suppositions which will be advanced from time to time in subsequent chapters in connection with some Ethiopian myths and legends for which confirmatory archeological evidence is still wanting. With these thoughts in mind, we may now turn our attention to the serious question of the important position of ancient Ethiopia in early European tradition.

A consideration of the origin and ancient meaning of the word Ethiopia provides a convenient and logical point of departure for this discussion, for it is significant that the expression is distinctly a European product. The ancient Ethiopians never called themselves Ethiopians or their land Ethiopia, nor did the ancient Egyptians or the early Hebrews ever make use of these terms in referring to their neighbors and contemporaries. The earliest mention of the word in surviving records is found in the first book of the *Iliad,* dating, it is generally thought, from the ninth century B.C.; but from that date on it was a rather commonly used term in the literature of the classical world.

Ethiopia, or Aethiopia, was for the early Greeks roughly equivalent to "the land of sun-burned or black-faced men." Use of the word in such a connection may have been current in Homer's day; but documentary proof of this is wanting, for it is true that Homer, unlike the later writers, nowhere specifically states that Ethiopia was the home of "sun-burned" or "black-faced" men. But, as we soon shall see, his linking the country so closely with the "rising and the setting sun" and referring specifically to its "warm limits" would seem to warrant the inference that he, like his successors, associated that land with "sun-burned" or "black-faced" men. A little further along in this chapter, it will be shown that, on the basis of archeological evidence, there are good grounds for believing that blacks from Africa had been domiciled in the Aegean lands hundreds of years before Homer's day, and that the type was certainly well represented in the area in the centuries immediately following the age in which the great poet lived. In this connection, it may be noted that in the passage in the *Odyssey* where Eurybates is mentioned as having "short woolly curls" and a "sabled-hue," there can hardly be any doubt that the poet is describing an Ethiopian, yet he does not specifically identify him as such. On the strength of such evidence, the suggestion may reasonably be made that the ebony hue of the Ethiopians was so well known in Homer's day that, as a poet, he hardly felt it necessary specifically to mention a fact so familiar to all.

How much did Homer and his contemporaries know about Ethiopia and the Ethiopians, how exact was their knowledge, what was the source of their information, and what were the opinions and the attitudes of these early Europeans towards the culture and customs of their distant and dusky contemporaries? It is only by an examination of the evidence and authoritative opinion in which these questions find their answers that we can arrive at any pronouncement of worth regarding the true position of ancient Ethiopia in early European tradition.

Concerning the question of the extent and the exactness of Homeric information relating to the Ethiopians, the traditional and orthodox opinion among scholars is that Homer, his contemporaries, and their immediate successors possessed but a very limited and hazy knowledge of the distant people and their country. Sir E. A. Budge's comment is typical: "A country and a people of whom neither he [Homer] nor his contemporaries had any exact knowledge." While one may accept in the main the general truth of this orthodox and conservative point of view, care must be taken not to accept it too literally lest some valuable sidelights on, first, the influence of early Ethiopian culture, and second, the origin of certain elements in European tradition be overlooked or ignored. Certain scholars, by committing just this error, have handicapped their own efforts to understand and explain what is one of the most fascinating problems that has come down to us from the ancient world, namely, the *raison d'être* for the honor and renown accredited to Ethiopia and the Ethiopians in the mythology and legends that grew up in the glorious Homeric age and in early classical times.

The classical literature treating Ethiopia may be divided into two general categories. The first includes the writings of certain of the Greek and Roman poets and dramatists, while the second is composed mainly of the works of certain celebrated historians, naturalists, and geographers. The writings in the first group treat, in the main, subjects of a rather legendary and mythological nature; while the information embodied in the works of the second group is concerned for the most part with matters, men, and events which are of a more definite and authenticated historical character. In the roster of authors making up the first group are some of the most celebrated names known to literature: among the poets are Homer, Hesiod, Pindar, Ovid, and Virgil; the dramatists include Aeschylus, Sophocles, and Euripides, while the romancers are represented by Pseudo-Callisthenes and Heliodorus of Emesa. The list of authors comprising the second group is no less distinguished: the historians being represented by Herodotus, Diodorus Siculus, Josephus, and Dion Cassius; the naturalists by Aristotle and Pliny the Elder, and the geographers by Claudius Ptolemy and the unknown author of *Periplus of the Erythraean Sea.*

These lists include, for the most part, only the names of some of the more noted classical authors whose notices and accounts of Ethiopia have been preserved for us in their own words. There are scores of other equally distinguished classical writers who are known to have written at considerable length concerning the famous African empire and its peoples but whose references are now preserved only through citations recorded in the works of others. In the course of this survey considerable attention will be given to certain of the writers in this class.

Although these notices of Ethiopia long have been known to students of classical literature and, after a fashion, to scholars interested in the history of antiquity, it is only within the past generation or so that the great body of these references has come to be recognized as having any real value as historical material. It is true that certain noted African travelers and students of Nilotic history—such as James Bruce, Count Volney, A. H. Heeren, and G. A. Hoskins—showed many years ago a disposition to accept the historical import of such materials, but the majority of scholars hesitated to accept their lead. This practice of ignoring or disregarding most of the references to Ethiopia found in the works of the classical authors resulted from the skeptical attitude taken toward the historical value of the classics by the Wolfian school of classical criticism, a skepticism which was furthered by the introduction of the so-called scientific method in the study of history by Leopold V. Ranke and his followers.

Under the influence of these developments, the classics in general as historical sources came to be hedged about with so many doubts and reservations that few historians dared to make serious use of them. Of later writers, such as Herodotus, Diodorus Siculus, and Pliny the Elder, a similar situation prevailed. It became the custom to regard the Homeric and the classical notices and traditions concerning the antiquity and grandeur of Ethiopian civilization as being hardly more than bits of poetic extravaganza and graceless fictions, which owed their origin almost solely to the fertile imagination of the Helladic mind. Especially was this the case with those citations found in the works of the earlier Greek authors.

In further justification of this general attitude, it was alleged that the earlier inhabitants of the Aegean world knew practically nothing of a trustworthy character concerning Ethiopia or the Ethiopians for the simple reason that there were no channels through which such information could reach them. It was further argued by some scholars that Greek acquaintance with the Ethiopian type hardly dated further back

than the fifth century B.C.—the occasion of the first direct contacts being the arrival of the Negro or Ethiopian soldiers who
accompanied Xerxes' army to Greece in the year 480. Other
scholars contended indeed that it was not until the third and
second centuries B.C. that the Greeks came to have any real
firsthand acquaintance with or any trustworthy knowledge of
Ethiopia and its peoples. These developments, it was alleged,
were first brought about through the commercial relations
with Ethiopia and the tours of exploration which were carried
out under the patronage of the Greek or the Ptolemaic dynasty which was then ruling in Egypt. Before the establishment
of such contacts, Ethiopia, it was claimed, was essentially a *terra incognita* to the inhabitants of the Aegean world. Hence,
such references and allusions to Ethiopia and the Ethiopians
as were contained in the works written before these dates
were hardly more than the embellishments of a few travelers'
tales, which doubtless had been passed on to the Aegean
writers by way of Phoenicia or Egypt. It was admitted that
later writers like Diodorus Siculus, Strabo, and Pliny the Elder
may have derived some of their information through more
direct and trustworthy channels. Yet, since these authors were
wont to draw heavily upon the traditions current long before
their day, it was the general practice of scholars to reject much
or most of what they too had to say concerning Ethiopia.
Thus, most of the notices of Ethiopia found in the works of
most of the classical authors were considered to be scarcely
worthy of serious attention by scholars in quest of solid facts
of history.

During the last century many things have happened
which have seriously modified the attitude of the historians.
First, the value of the classics in general as historical sources
has been enhanced. Second and more specifically, it has been
much demonstrated that Aegean and Ethiopian contacts were
more ancient and more direct than was previously thought. A

brief recapitulation of the discoveries and developments which have brought about these changed attitudes will contribute materially to a fuller appreciation of the historical value of the references to Ethiopia in the classical sources under review. We shall consider first those discoveries and developments which have tended to restore the classics in general to favor as valuable sources of historical materials.

Before the last quarter of the nineteenth century, it was the general practice of historians to think of Aegean, or more properly, Greek civilization and the traditions associated with it, as being essentially indigenous products of a relatively late origin. It has been suggested that the first Olympiad, traditionally dated in 776 B.C., might well be taken as the starting point of Greek history. The traditions embodied in the Homeric poems and in the poems of the epic cycle, which purported to relate to personages, things, and events alleged to have been a part of the history of older civilizations that once had flourished in the Aegean land, had, it was generally supposed, no real foundation in fact. The rape of Helen and the chagrin of Menelaus; the grand attack on Troy and the ebb and flow of fortune in the siege; the wooden horse and the fall of the city; the wanderings of Odysseus and the quest of Telemachus for his much-afflicted father; the faithfulness of Penelope in the midst of the wicked suitors and the reunion of old Argus with his long-suffering master—these and similar stirring and touching episodes, no less than such references to ancient cities as "rich Mycenae," "Tiryns of Great Walls," and "Knossos the City in which Minos reigned" were all alike regarded by most scholars as figments of bardic imagination practically devoid of any ground in historic truth.

But Heinrich Schliemann, a German, was destined to revolutionize the prevailing interpretations placed on the relations of these traditions to Greek history. He was to pave the way for a complete reevaluation of the classics as historical sources, a major contribution for subsequent researchers.

Schliemann not only became convinced that Troy, Mycenae, Tiryns, and the other cities mentioned in the Homeric poems had really existed as great metropolises but also believed that their remains could be found by excavating the sites where they were alleged by the ancients to have stood; and he was resolved sooner or later to demonstrate the truth of his views to a skeptical world. Beginning in 1871 he electrified the public by laying bare, from beneath tons of debris of gigantic ruins, remains which were of such a character that even the most doubtful critics could not deny that Schliemann had indeed found the site of ancient Troy. Flushed by this brilliant confirmation of his faith in the historical bases of the central theme in Homeric legends, Schliemann next went to Greece in quest of other cities immortalized in the incomparable lines of the Prince of Poets, and in 1876 again startled the world by one of the most remarkable archeological finds of all time, the shaft-graves located on the Acropolis of Homer's "rich Mycenes," the city over which the great Agamemnon had reigned. Again, in 1880, he discovered at Orchomenos—which according to tradition was the last resting place of the bones of Hesiod—the so-called Treasury of Mingas; and four years later he laid bare the foundations of a great prehistoric palace which once had stood in Homer's "Tiryns of Great Walls." Though Schliemann misinterpreted some of his finds and did not live long enough to realize the full import of these remarkable discoveries which had opened up to the historian a new world, sufficient years were spared him to enjoy being universally acclaimed as the first to prove that the Homeric legends were based upon real facts. The full significance of Schliemann's discoveries was not thoroughly established until many years after his death. This was the achievement of later scholars, who followed up and expanded the excavations which Schliemann had begun with such industry and such magnificent faith.

The high water mark in these developments was reached in the monumental excavations carried out in Crete by Sir Arthur Evans during the first quarter of the present century. Through these excavations, supplemented by similar operations by other investigators in the Cyclades, in Asia Minor, and on mainland Greece, it has been shown first that there once flourished throughout the Aegean Sea and its environs an old and brilliant civilization whose beginnings dated back to about 3000 B.C.; second, that the fountainhead of this remarkable culture centered in the island of Crete; third, that at various intervals in the long history of this civilization there were apparently some very direct contacts between the peoples who established and maintained it and certain of the peoples of Africa; fourth, that the ruins and remains which Schliemann discovered at Troy, Orchomenos, Mycenae, and Tiryns, and which are generally designated as the Mycenaean cultures, are of a relatively late phase of this civilization; and fifth, that this old civilization, through the agency of the Mycenaean culture-complex, exercised a profound influence upon the material and literary aspects of the Greek civilization of historic times.

A certain Homeric passage holds that "Knossos [was] the city in which Minos reigned"; and according to Thucydides it was Minos of Knossos who paved the way for the development of a high and stable civilization in the Aegean area by driving the pirates from the sea. Strabo credits this king with having invented the science of jurisprudence and states that it was from Crete that came the basic ideas and practices that characterized the laws of the ancient Greeks. For many years these ancient traditions were scoffed at by scholars as having no foundation in fact, but the brilliant discoveries of Sir Arthur Evans revealed an abundance of evidence which seems

to indicate that these traditions were quite sound, for in the
course of his excavations he discovered the ruins of a city
which correspond in an admirable way to the descriptions of
Knossos preserved in the Homeric and later traditions.

Sir Arthur Evans designated that old and long-lived culture, which centered in Crete and was radiated throughout
the Aegean area, as the Minoan civilization, after the much
celebrated Cretan ruler King Minos. Archeological synchro-
nisms made it possible to establish links between prehistoric
Crete and ancient Egypt. Sir Arthur Evans divided the chronology into three main periods: the Early Minoan, extending
roughly from circa 3400 to 2100 B.C.; the Middle Minoan, c.
2100 to 1580 B.C., and the Late Minoan or the Mycenaean, c.
1580 to 1200 B.C. It was during the latter part of the second and
the early part of the third periods that Minoan influences
made their impress upon the peoples and cultures which
played such an important part in the legends of the Homeric
age.

From the foregoing considerations two very significant
facts clearly emerge: first, that Greek civilization was not fun-
damentally an indigenous product dating, as older historians
believed, from the eighth century B.C. or about the time of the
first Olympiad; and second, that traditions preserved in
Homeric legends and later works based upon them were
founded upon events which had considerable foundation in
fact. Such, then, in brief outline is the story of those discoveries which have contributed so much in restoring the earlier of
the classics to favor as valuable sources of historical materials.

## THE AEGEAN AND AFRICA

 e may now turn our attention to the second
aspect of this essay, namely, those discoveries
and developments which have tended to estab-

lish the fact that the early peoples of the Aegean, who figured prominently in the origin of the Homeric traditions, were in much closer contacts with the peoples of Africa than was previously thought. The purpose of this discussion is to show that the references and allusions to Ethiopia and the Ethiopians found in the earlier classical sources were not necessarily based upon hearsay tales borrowed by the early Greeks from the Phoenicians and Egyptians, but may have grown out of much more ancient and direct contacts.

The word Ethiopia was of early Greek origin; it frequently appears in the Homeric poems, the oldest forms of Greek literature that have come down to us, and was apparently in use long before these poems were composed. Attention has also been called to the fact that up until very recently it was the opinion of most scholars that the land and peoples referred to in this connection were only vaguely and hazily known to the earlier peoples of the Aegean area, that there were no direct contacts between the Aegean and the black or Ethiopian peoples until the fifth or possibly the third and second centuries B.C.; hence the references and allusions to Ethiopia and the Ethiopians contained in the earlier forms of Aegean or Greek literature were probably based upon purely hearsay traditions and were as a consequence of little if any historical value. Discoveries and studies connected with the early Minoan civilization, supplemented by other more or less directly associated finds and observations, have yielded much evidence that there were some very intimate and extensive contacts between the Ethiopian peoples and the peoples of the Aegean or Minoan world. The considerations which may be brought forward in this connection can be divided into two general categories: first, those based on certain very ancient traditions preserved in the works of certain classical authors; and second, those growing out of relatively recent archeological discoveries and anthropological studies made in both the Aegean area and several places in northeastern Africa.

Concerning the first group of considerations, the following observations may be made. Diodorus Siculus, who has preserved the fullest accounts of the older legends current in the
ancient Aegean world, relates a tradition that the very ancient
peoples of inner Africa were famed as valiant warriors and
"used to send great forces abroad into other countries where
they succeeded in bringing many parts of the world under
their dominion." Diodorus based his story on "many things
reported of them by both the Ancients and historians," and
gave a particularly long and interesting account of one allegedly very ancient African people who were especially celebrated for exploits abroad. This account relates that "long
before the Trojan War" there was situated in western Africa
"on the borders of Ethiopia" a nation which was ruled by a
long line of powerful female sovereigns, and that under the
leadership of one of these, an Amazonian queen named Mer-
ina, there arose a large army which not only overran vast
regions of northern Africa and western Asia but also conquered many islands in the Mediterranean Sea. Crete, the
center of the early Minoan culture, is not specifically mentioned, but the traditions do relate that it was through these
conquests that Corybantes (the eponymous ancestors of Idaei
Dactyli and Curetes, the earliest civilized inhabitants of Crete)
came to be established in this island world.

Diodorus also records another tradition that several generations later internal distubances in Africa caused "Ammon, a
king reigning in some part of Libya, to flee into Crete where
he married Geta, one of the daughters of the Cretes then
reigning there and through her gained the sovereignty of the
Island." And the celebrated story of Atlantis, preserved by
Plato in the *Critias* and in the *Timaeus*, tells us that Atlantian
traditions affirmed that conquerors from Atlantis at one time
"subjected to their rule the inland parts of Libya [Greek name

for Africa west of the Nile] as far as Egypt," if not beyond.

There is a disposition on the part of certain modern scholars to identify the famed Atlantis of ancient tradition with Minoan Crete. If Atlantis and Minoan Crete were one and the same—and it must be confessed that the proponents of this view seem to have established a very good case—it would appear, on the strength of the foregoing citations from Diodorus and Plato, that the ancient peoples of the Aegean world possessed traditions of some far-reaching conflicts and extensive intercommunications between themselves and the peoples of inner Africa.

Summarizing the general import of the discoveries made by Schliemann, Evans, and others in the Aegean area, it should be noted that evidence was found which seemed to indicate that at various intervals in the long history of Minoan civilization there were evidently direct contacts with peoples and cultures of black or African origin. Evidence of such intercommunications dates from the very beginnings of the early Minoan civilization: along the southern coasts of Crete in the Missara Plain and at Mochlos in the eastern part of the island. Furthermore, in certain of the islands of the Cyclades, the Cretan archeologist Stephanos Xantherdides, Sir Arthur Evans, and others have discovered and explored a series of "beehive" or "hut" tombs belonging, according to Sir Arthur, to the very earliest stage of Minoan civilization. These Aegean ossuaries, as Sir Arthur further points out, bear striking resemblances to a type of very ancient tomb structure that had a wide distribution throughout Africa—namely in proto-dynastic Egypt, Libya, the western Sahara, the Sudan, and Ethiopia. He further believes that this type of tomb had its origin in Africa and was introduced into the Aegean area by emigrants from Africa. Moreover, certain of the objects found in these tombs, including types of pottery, stone idols, beautifully carved stone vases, and foot-shaped emulets, also find striking parallels in similar Libyan and Egyptian objects dating from the pre-dynastic and proto-dynastic periods.

One of the objects mentioned is of particular significance for our immediate discussion. This is a fragment of seashell carved in the shape of a human head, the face of which is characterized by a "snub nose and thick tumid lips." Indeed a casual glance at the object leads one at once to the conclusion that the artist who carved the piece was without question attempting to represent a member of the black race, and as Sir Arthur says, this fact clearly indicates that the people associated with the culture of this period must have had some "contact with an ethnic ingredient of Negroid affinity." Moreover, the shell belongs, according to its discoverer, to a species of shellfish whose nearest habitat must have been the African littoral along the Red Sea coast.

The points of resemblance between the earliest Minoan culture and that of early Egypt, Libya, and other parts of Africa led Sir Arthur, the ranking authority on the subject, to attribute the foundation of Early Minoan culture to an actual settlement of colonists from North Africa in Crete. These considerations, along with research which has shown that there was a large black or Negroid element in North Africa in the proto-dynastic period of Egypt and, above all, the Negroid head represented on the shell mentioned, would seem to indicate that the peoples associated with the Minoan culture were acquainted with the Ethiopian type from the very beginning of the Minoan age.

Evidence indicating contact between the Aegean area and Africa and Minoan acquaintance with the Ethiopian type, is likewise available for the Middle Minoan period. In Egypt Professors W. M. F. Petrie and John Garstang discovered Aegean or Cretan pottery in association with native cultural remains which belong to a period contemporary with the Middle Minoan period, and in Crete Sir Arthur Evans found

Egyptian objects dating from the same age. Again, Sir Arthur pointed out that the dress and the methods of headdress of the peoples of the Middle Minoan period bear some interesting and detailed analogies to those of the early Nilotic peoples and the ancient Libyans. Sir Arthur further pointed out that the bow and arrow and the eight-sided shield of the very late Middle Minoan period, as represented in the Minoan hieroglyphics and on seal stones, show close resemblances to similar weapons represented in ancient Libyan and Saharan rock carvings, and are still found in use among certain of the present-day peoples of East Africa.

Other instances of similar import could be given, but enough has been said to make it clear that there was evidently some kind of contact between the ancient Minoan and the ancient African cultures. That at least some of the African peoples involved in these contacts were of an Ethiopian affinity is strongly suggested by the following facts. Sir Arthur, in the course of excavating at Knossos, came upon some faience fragments on which are portrayed a number of individuals whom he considered as belonging to a Negroid or Ethiopian folk. This is indicated by their physical features, for they have "a prognathous face and swarthy color," and the body is characterized by "an abdominal prominence and a tendency to the steatopygous rump." Whether the individuals represented here were actually on Cretan soil or whether they were figured to memorialize members of the race seen in Africa is an uncertainty, but Sir Arthur was inclined to favor the latter possibility.

From what part of Africa these people might have come our author does not dare to suggest, but an observation or two might be hazarded on this point. The fact that these individuals are seemingly characterized by that peculiar physical character, steatopygia, seems to point in the general direction of Ethiopia or at least to the regions south of Egypt and the Sahara. Peoples distinguished by this trait seemingly have existed in the Ethiopian area for thousands of years; they are frequently represented on the Ethiopian monuments of the Meroitic period—c. 750 B.C.–350 A.D. And from the days of Sir Richard Burton down to our own time, the prominence of this feature among some of the people, the women in particular, has hardly escaped the eye of a single observant traveler in these parts.

In the course of the same excavations, Sir Arthur also found a fragment of pointed stucco relief, assigned to the Middle Minoan period, showing "a man's hand fingering a gold necklace with heads of Negroid affinity." The hair is black and curly, the eyes large, the lips thick and the nose short and broad. The skin color, however, is represented as a "tawny yellow," a fact which led Sir Arthur to suggest that the heads of the original necklace were probably of gold. The prove-nance of the original necklace and of the ethnic type it represents is of course unknown, but the fact that the heads of the original necklace were in all likelihood of gold seems to point, as Sir Arthur observes, to Ethiopia or some neighboring African country as the source of at least the precious metal; and it may be suggested that it is even more probable that the same regions supplied the human models after which the heads were patterned.

As interesting and significant as are the foregoing facts and observations, it is nevertheless from ruins belonging to the Late Minoan period that the most important body of evidence indicating Aegean and African contacts have come. Perhaps the best known and the most significant object in this series is a large fragment of fresco painting, found by Sir Arthur at Knossos, representing a red-skinned or brown-skinned Cretan or Minoan officer leading a troop of Negroes. This most interesting painting has been given by its discoverer the appropriate title, "The Minoan Captain of the Blacks." Associated with this fresco were two others of the same technical character depicting a garden scene in which baboons belonging to a well-known central African variety (Cercopithecus Calletrichus) are gamboling about in a growth of plants and flowers. In addition to these remains there have also been found in the ruins of Crete considerable quantities of ivory fragments, ostrich eggshells, gold, and gold dust; and since none of these materials are native to Crete but are plentiful in the interior of Africa, it has been suggested that they were in all probability of central African origin.

In the opinion of Sir Arthur Evans, through whose labors they were brought to light, the various objects and products enumerated almost certainly indicate extensive contacts between the civilization of Minoan Crete and inner Africa. Some of the products mentioned may have found their way into Crete by way of the Nile valley and Egypt, but he also points out that certain evidence exists which suggests connections with the interior of the continent by overland routes across the Sahara. "We may well believe," he concluded, "that it was by these routes at least, as much as through the Nile Valley, that such exotic products as ivory, ostrich egg shells, gold dust and some, perhaps, of the long tailed Sudan monkeys reached the Southern havens of Crete."

In connection with Sir Arthur's postulates about trade routes across the Sahara at this period, it may be pointed out that there is now considerable evidence to indicate that this part of Africa was by no means so dry in ancient times as it is today; hence trade and travel between the African interior and the Mediterranean world well might have been carried on in Minoan times with much less effort and peril than now attend undertakings of this kind.

The blacks represented on the plaques and in the paintings are extremely significant, for here we seem to have clear evidence that the Ethiopian type was well known in Crete during this period. The fresco showing the Minoan general leading black soldiers is thought to be particularly important, for this painting belongs to the very period in Cretan history —the sixteenth and fifteenth centuries B.C.—when Minoan imperialism and overseas expansion were at their height, and Minoan civilization was being established throughout the eastern Mediterranean basin. On the strength of this painting it is not too much to suggest that Ethiopian auxiliaries took a prominent part in the military operations growing out of these undertakings, and it is quite possible that the Minoan commanders, like the Egyptian pharaohs in their imperial endeavors, "made use of black regiments for the final conquest of a large part of the Peloponnese and Mainland Greece." In this connection it is interesting to note that there have been discovered in Illyria and in the Balkans certain skeletons and statuettes from this general period which are said to be characterized by Negro and Negroid traits.

In the Greek legends, there is a story that the Peloponnese, or ancient Sparta, was originally given by Zeus to Heracles (Hercules) and his descendants, the Heraclidae, but through the chicanery of Hera, the Heraclidae were for a time deprived of their patrimony and forced to live in a region to the northwest (in the vicinity of Illyria); later they succeeded in winning by force of arms the mastery of the territory. The recovery of the Peloponnese is known in the legend as the "Return of the Heraclidae", and in history is closely bound up with the invasions of the Dorians. In classical times the Peloponnese was the main seat of the Dorians, the most powerful representatives of which were the Spartans. It has become customary to look upon the Dorians as one of the great divisions of the Hellenic stock, and their center of origin is generally placed in Macedonia or Epirus; but it is a curious fact that the oldest literary references to them (in the *Odyssey*) mention them as a southern people dwelling in the islands of

Crete and Rhodes, a fact which long has puzzled classical scholars.

Interesting also is the fact that in the drawing on the famous Caeretan hydra (which preserves one of the very earliest attempts to depict the celebrated Hera) representing an incident in the legend of Hercules' African encounter with Busiris, Hercules' features are given a peculiarly Ethiopian cast; and again in one of the so-called Homeric hymns, "The Cercopes," where a daughter of the legendary Ethiopian king, Memnon, warns her sons to keep away from Hercules, Hercules is given the sobriquet "Blackbottom." Hence, in the traditions of very ancient times it would seem that Hercules, regarded as the eponymous ancestor of certain of the Spartans, was in one way or another associated with Africa and the Ethiopian type.

There can be little doubt that the actual archeological remains mentioned—particularly the ivory, the ostrich eggshells, the representations of blacks on the shell, the faience and fresco fragments, and finally the Negroid skeletons and statuettes discovered in and about the confines of the old Minoan Empire—clearly indicate the existence of intercommunications between Ethiopian and Aegean peoples dating back to a very ancient period. Since the discoveries of Schliemann, Evans, and other investigators have established that the themes of the Homeric poems were founded to a considerable extent upon traditions which had their origin in actual historical occurrences of the Minoan periods, and since it has been shown that more or less direct intercommunications existed between the Aegean peoples and peoples of an Ethiopian type throughout these periods, it seems reasonably safe to conclude that the old opinion, which held that the Homeric reference to Ethiopia and the Ethiopians was based upon hearsay tales borrowed by the Homeric writers from Egyptians or Phoenicians, must be accepted with a great deal of reservation, if indeed not rejected altogether.

The considerations hitherto brought forward bear in the main upon the problem of the sources or origins of the Ethiopian notices found in the earlier of the Greek writings, to the poems belonging to the Homeric Age and Age of the Epic Cycle, including particularly the poems of Homer, Hesiod, and Arctinus of Miletus, all of which were composed between the tenth and seventh centuries B.C. There is considerable evidence which indicates that the Greeks of the late transitional and the early classical ages—of the seventh, sixth, and fifth centuries B.C., when Hecataeus, Aeschylus, Euripides, and Herodotus made their references to Ethiopia—were definitely and directly acquainted with the Ethiopian type. This view, it will be perceived, is contrary to the widely held opinion that direct Greek acquaintance with the Ethiopian type dated no further back than the time of Xerxes' invasion of Greece in the fifth century B.C., and that it was their deep impression on the Greek mind which made them the fashion of classical Greek culture. Other scholars believe the Ethiopian presence dates only from the time of the Ptolemaic dominion in Egypt in the third and second centuries B.C.

The evidence upon which this chain of post-Homeric Graeco-Ethiopian interrelationships is based is, in the, main archeological and has been assembled from widely scattered Greek sites in and about the eastern end of the Mediterranean basin. It may be said at once that these materials seem to indicate that there was a relatively large black population in the Greek world throughout these ages. But it is now believed that the presence of black Africans in Europe antedates the fifth century by thousands of years. Twentieth century archeology has revealed, for example, that there were blacks in Europe as early as the Aurignacian phase of the Paleolithic epoch or Old Stone Age, that is, as early as twenty to thirty thousand years ago. Basing their conclusions on the discovery of the skeletons in the *Grotte des Enfants* on the Franco-Italian frontier and on the Negroid affinities of some of the skeletons ascribed to the Cro-Magnon race, as well as the Africanoid elements in much of the celebrated Aurignacian art, eminent prehistorians like René Verneau, William J. Sollas, and Marcellin Boule have declared that the black race evidently constituted an influential and widespread part of the population of Europe in those far away times.* According to many eminent authorities, traces of this ancient race are to be detected throughout the later and closing phases of the Old Stone Age in Europe, and in the Neolithic Age as well. France, Spain, Switzerland, and Central Europe all have yielded skeletal remains in which many of Europe's ablest paleontologists profess to see traces of the Negro type.

For our purposes, however, it will be sufficient to restrict our attention to evidence indicating the presence of Africans in the regions around the eastern part of the Mediterranean basin, between the beginning of the second millennium before Christ and the epogee of the classical age. This was the area and the time in which the myths and legends with which we are concerned had their rise. Evidence pointing to the presence of the Ethiopian type in this general area for this period has been recorded from Crete, Illyria and its hinterlands, Cyprus, Rhodes, Aegina, Caere, and Attica, and from Cyrenaica and the early Greek city of Naukratis on the north African coast. It is not implied, of course, that evidence is available to indicate that blacks were continually present or always known in these several communities throughout that long period, far from it. Indeed, some of the sites are represented only by a single find, and for the sites where the finds are more numerous, they are sometimes separated by several

---

*See also the thesis of Chester Chand, "Implications of Early Human Migrations from Africa to Europe," *Man*, v. 63, no. 152 (August 1963), p. 124.—Ed.

hundred years. It is only fair to say, however, that the material recorded to date constitutes in all probability but a frac-
tion of that which once existed on these several sites. With
these qualifying thoughts in mind, we may now turn our attention to a brief survey of that evidence which seems to
point to a long and relatively close acquaintance of the myth-
creating peoples of the Aegean area with the folks and things
of Ethiopian or inner African origin.

To some of our modern scholars, among them the great
George Grote, Minos and his capital at Knossos paved the way
for the high civilization in the Aegean around Crete. Wilhelm
Dorpfeld, David G. Hogarth, Schliemann, and Sir Arthur
Evans have demonstrated that Minos and Knossos were ac-
tualities and have proved that Crete was, as ancient legend
and traditions affirmed, indeed the chief center from which
were radiated those influences which brought the first true
civilization to Europe. The main outlines of these dramatic archeological discoveries are now well and widely known; they
constitute a stock possession in the knowledge of every
student of ancient history. All popular works, and every high
school and college textbook treating of Europe in historical
antiquity, manage to include accounts of the major facts and
finds which point to the Minoan or Cretan beginning of those
cultures and traditions which culminated in the glory that was
Greece. But however this may be, few of these secondary
works find it convenient to include, or even allude to, the fact
that the same discoveries which have confirmed the traditional connections between the early civilizations of Europe and
ancient Crete have also revealed certain evidence which seems
to connect Ethiopia or black Africa with ancient Crete. Indeed,
the evidence seems to indicate that the links between the Ethiopian regions and Minoan Crete are not only older than the
links between Minoan Crete and mainland Greece or Europe
but that it was with the aid of Ethiopians that Cretan culture

was first carried to the coasts of Europe, and then inland.

The oldest bit of evidence suggesting a connection between a Cretan and an Ethiopian area was discovered by Sir Arthur Evans near Phaeton in 1894. This was a fragment of seashell carved in the shape of a human head, the face of which is characterized by a "snub nose and thick tumid lips." Indeed, a casual glance at the object leads one to the conclusion that the artist or artisan who carved the piece was without question attempting to represent a black African. The age of the fragment is uncertain, but Sir Arthur, impressed by the resemblance of the head to certain Negroid heads represented on Egyptian slate palettes dating from the pre-Dynastic Age in Egypt, concluded that the fragment probably belonged to the Early Minoan Age in Crete. Whether or not the object was made in Crete or imported from some African area is not known; but as Sir Arthur pointed out, there are very good grounds for believing that there were strong currents from the North African coast—particularly it seems, from Libya and Egypt. Moreover, the shell belongs to a species of shellfish whose nearest habitat must have been the African littoral along the Red Sea coast. These conclusions are significant, for as the researches of D. R. MacIver and C. G. Seligman, and other investigators have shown, there was a large black population in Egypt in the pre-Dynastic Age and it is also further known that the end of the pre-Dynastic Age was characterized by the migrations into Egypt of still other blacks from the inner regions of Africa.

Of more importance than this isolated head are a series of more or less similar objects associated with the later and greater phases of Cretan civilization. There are some fragmentary stucco and faience plaques and panels, discovered by Sir Arthur Evans at Knossos, depicting scenes in which Negroes occupy a prominent if not the leading part. The earliest of these, some faience fragments found with the so-called

Town Mosaic and dating from the Middle Minoan II period (1900–1700 B.C.), portray a number of individuals which Sir Arthur considers as belonging to a black or Negroid folk. This is indicated, he thinks, by the Negro-like aspect of their physical features, for they have "a prognathous face, and the body is characterized by an abdominal prominence and tendency to the steatopygous rump." Whether the individuals represented here were modeled after blacks or Negroids on Cretan soil as mentioned previously or whether they were figured to memorialize members of the race seen in Africa, is an uncertainty; so both possibilities exist.

The next object in the series from Knossos is a rather large fragment of fresco painting representing a red-skinned Cretan or Minoan officer leading a troop of blacks. This significant fragment, mentioned previously and quite appropriately called "The Minoan Captain of the Blacks," is thought to belong to the Late Minoan I or possibly to the Late Minoan II period; its tentative date, therefore, is somewhere between 1580 and 1400 B.C. This fragment is by all odds the most significant of the entire lot from Knossos, for here we seem to have almost certain proof of the presence of Negroes in Crete at this all-important stage in Cretan history. Concerning their functions, Sir Arthur has advanced two suggestions, the first that they possibly constituted the Palace Guard; and the second that they might have served as auxiliaries in the Minoan imperial army. It is known from other evidence that it was at just this period that Minoan imperialism and overseas expansion were at their height, and it is reasonable to assume, as Sir Arthur thinks, that Ethiopian auxiliaries took a prominent part in the military operations growing out of these undertakings.

In the periods of the Old, Middle, and New Kingdoms of ancient Egypt, the military prowess of Ethiopian soldiers figured most prominently in the imperial endeavors of the

Egyptian pharaohs and the warlords of Knossos, and the kings of Crete seem to have followed a similar practice. With such thoughts in mind, and with the Cretan evidence before him, Sir Arthur concluded that it was probable that the "Minoan Commanders made use of black regiments for the final conquest of a large part of the Peloponnese and mainland Greece." During this period in Cretan expansion, Minoan culture and influence were established not only in the Peloponnese and mainland Greece but were radiated with increasing force to outlying areas, including the Troy or the Troad and the coastal region of Thessaly. To what extent Negro troops were used, if at all, we do not know, but it is significant that certain evidence indicating the presence of Negroes in some of these outlying areas has come to light. For example, in 1919 N. M. Zupanic reported in *Revue Anthropologique* that there had been discovered in Illyria and in the Balkans certain skeletons and statuettes which are said to be characterized by Negroid traits. The age of these finds, like objects belonging to all prehistoric culture, can only be approximately determined; but the reported opinion is that they apparently belong to the Late Neolithic or the Eneolithic periods.

By assuming, as we may, that the Late Neolithic and the Eneolithic cultures of Illyria and the Balkans survived until a relatively late date (to a time when the Bronze Age was already well established in Crete), we can bring these Thessalian finds within the date limits assigned for the Minoan period. If these suppositions be allowed, they tend to broaden and strengthen Sir Arthur's suggestion that the Minoan commanders may have made use of black regiments. It is indeed highly improbable that an island no larger than Crete could have supplied, from its limited and seemingly luxury-loving populace, the large number of soldiers required to establish and maintain Minoan dominion over the vast and scattered areas which seem to have been under its rule. Like their Egyptian contemporaries, the Cretans may be supposed to have augmented their ranks and provided for the distant garrisons by recruiting among Ethiopians. With the collapse of Crete, the heart of the Minoan empire, around 1400 B.C., the Ethiopians, particularly those in the distant outposts of the empire, would have been left to shift for themselves. Some may have sought to return to their own country.

There are yet some additional finds from Knossos which serve to strengthen further the postulate of Cretan and inner African relationships. These are two fragments of painted frescoe panels depicting monkeys gamboling about among flowers and papyrus stalks. Sir Arthur Evans thinks these panels are of the same approximate date as the "Captain of the Blacks," and he identifies the monkeys as members of the African baboon family whose habitat at the present day is in the tropical forest of the western Sudan. The baboons of the Cretan frescoes, says Sir Arthur, are the same "green monkeys" imported by the ancient Egyptians from Ethiopia and its environs and which were popular as pets and playthings of Egypt's women. It is possible, as Sir Arthur points out, that the Cretans may have derived their familiarity with these African monkeys by way of Egypt; but he also calls attention to evidence which suggests possible connections between Crete and the inner regions of Africa by overland routes across the Sahara, and noted: "We may well believe that it was by these routes, at least as much as through the Nile Valley, that such exotic products as ivory, ostrich egg shells, gold dust and perhaps some of the long tailed Sudan monkeys reached the southern havens of Crete."

It may also be noted that there is now available evidence which indicates that this part of Africa was by no means so dry in ancient times as it is today. Hence, trade and travel between the Sudan and North Africa might well have been carried on in Minoan times with less effort and peril than now. Furthermore, though specific evidence is as yet wanting, it is nevertheless highly probable that the great Minoan maritime merchants, like those of Phoenicia and Greece in later times, had ports of call if not permanent settlements along the North African coast, and by this means products as well as peoples may have traveled over the trade routes from the Sudan.

In the Classical Age, if the analysts of the time can be believed, a host of Greeks on their own initiative made the lengthy journey to "Meroe City of the Ethiopian" or at least to the kingdom over which it held sway. Pliny alone lists five such hardy wanderers—Dalion, Aristocreon, Simonides, Baeilis and Bion—and Diodorus records that Democritus of Abdera did the same. Indeed, there is a Greek tradition that Alexander the Great turned aside from his world-conquering campaign for a brief respite in the spinning palace of a sagacious queen of the Ethiopians. As we have already seen, modern archeology has practically established the truth of Herodotus' account of the African journey made by Cambyses' emissaries in quest of Ethiopia's far-famed "Table of the Sun."

Ethiopian relations with foreigners also occurred in conflicts beyond her borders, indeed, beyond the boundaries of her continent, and are recorded in certain annals of whose authenticity there can be little question. Ethiopia aided in the expulsion of the Asian Hyksos from Egypt, and Amenhotep III garrisoned Jerusalem with legions from Kush. And let us remember the implications of the Minoan frescoe, "The Captain of the Blacks"; and it will be remembered that these and other parallel instances occurred centuries before the Mycenaean period. And for the age which followed there is, in Africa, Piankhy's invasion (eighth century B.C.), which carried the standards of Ethiopia high throughout the length and breadth of Egypt and extended the boundaries of the Ethiopian empire as far northward as the "Great Green Sea."

For instances in which the clang of Ethiopian arms were to be heard in affrays occurring beyond the African continent, there might be cited the Hebrew accounts of how "it came to pass in the fifth year of King Rehoboam . . . Shishak king of Egypt with an army composed of the Lubims, the Sukiims and the Ethiopians . . . took the fenced cities which pertained to Judah . . . and came up against Jerusalem." Or, again, it might be related how in Judah when "Abijah slept with his fathers . . . there came out against them Zerah the Ethiopian with a host of a thousand and three hundred chariots." Finally, as a further instance of Ethiopia's participation in the arena of international affairs, there may be placed on record the heroic, if unsuccessful, efforts of "Tirhakah, King of Ethiopia" with Sennacherib and Esarhaddon to aid Judah, Tyre, and Sidon against mighty Assyria. If Ethiopian arms could, as they most assuredly did, figure so prominently in international and intercontinental affairs so long before and so soon after the siege of Troy, is it then not possible to believe, as the ancient accounts affirm, that the same could have occurred in the Mycenaean Age?

Additional information on Ethiopian and Egyptian relationships during the Seventeenth and Eighteenth Dynasties, made available through discoveries of the Kames Papyrus and the stele of Amonrenas and the finding of Ethiopian pottery in forts in Egypt, make it almost certain that the expulsion of the Hyksos and the establishment of the Eighteenth Dynasty were in large measure made possible by aid from Ethiopia; they indicate an almost certain Ethiopian origin of important members of the founders of the Eighteenth Dynasty. Thus the relationships existing between Crete, Late Minoan II, Troy VI, and Eighteenth Dynasty Egypt were relationships with a more or less Ethiopianized royal house.

Ashmes ı, who with his Ethiopian wife, was the founder of this great house, is known to have initiated conquests in western Asia, which under later rulers of that dynasty were to be so extended that the boundaries of the Egyptian empire reached as far eastward as Mesopotamia on the western borders of Persia. Amenhotep III, a particularly Ethiopian-looking prince of this house, numbered among his several wives two Asian princesses, one from Babylon and one from Mitani, both kingdoms in the neighborhood of Persia. And Amenhotep IV, the Negroid-appearing son of Amenhotep III and his great queen Tye, also of a decidedly Ethiopian appearance, is likewise known to have married a Mitanian princess. Thus the Egyptian royal family was most certainly related to the ruling houses of Ethiopia and probably to the ruling families of Troy and Minoan Crete.

As has been stated already, the ancient Greek notion that "burnt-faced men," or Ethiopians, existed in western and southern Asia seems, in the light of modern archeological research, to have much to substantiate it. The ancient Dravidians of India and the early populations of Persia and the southern Mesopotamian area seem also to have belonged to a black-skinned, wide-nosed, and woolly-haired race. According to Sir Arthur Keith's report on the Mount Carmel excavations to the Royal College of Surgeons, the same seems to have been the case in the Palestinian area from very ancient times until well into the second millennium B.C. The ultimate origin and the date of the coming of these Negroids to Asia are questions to which no satisfactory answer can now be given, but it may be suggested that at least some of them made their way into the eastern continent from Africa as early as late Paleolithic and early Neolithic times. They were doubtless forced to undertake this eastward migration as a consequence of the increasing dessication of the Saharan area of Africa, which seems to have been progressive after the closing phases of the Pleistocene period. But no matter what the cause or causes or the dates of its coming to Asia may have been, this type seems

to have been pretty well established in southwestern Asia in
the beginnings of historic times. And the great Dravidian,
Sumerian, and early Chaldean cultures, which were flourishing in that sector at that time, were undoubtedly largely the
products of its genius.

The spread of the Aryan and the rise and spread of the
Semitic and Mongolian peoples during the third and second
millennium B.C. came into serious competition with the older
black population, and in the clashes and racial intermixture
which followed, distinctive black cultural and ethnic traits
were considerably dissipated. In some regions the original features were more definitely preserved; the Persian area and its
environs seems to have been one of these. In Persia the old
Negroid element seems indeed to have been sufficiently
powerful to maintain the overlordship of the land. For the
Negritic strain is clearly evident in statuary depicting members of the royal family ruling in the second millennium B.C.

Hundreds of years later, when Xerxes invaded Greece, the
type was well represented in the Persian army. In the remote
mountain regions bordering on Persia and Baluchistan, there
is to be found at the present time a Negroid element which
bears a remarkable resemblance to the type represented on the
ancient monuments. Hence the Negritic or Ethiopian type has
proved persistent in this area, and in ancient times it seems to
have constituted numerically and socially an important factor
in the population. Whether the Ethiopian element of the first
and second millennium B.C. was entirely descended from the
old prehistoric type, or was reinforced by emigrants from
Africa, is not known, but it is by no means improbable that
the latter was the case. Throughout the third, second, and first
milenniums B.C., Ethiopia and its environs are known to have
been the seat of a particularly virile and energetic population,
which not only suppplied the Pharaohs of Egypt with the soldiers on which the Egyptian empire was largely built and

maintained but also at times, acting on initiative and forces from within, became a center from which was radiated great tidal waves of peoples who profoundly modified the politico-ethnic complex of the whole of the northeastern part of the African continent. Time and again these immigrants threatened to inundate Egypt; indeed, Egyptian evidence shows that on more than one occasion this very thing did happen.

The greatest movements of this kind occurred in the closing centuries of the third and the opening centuries of the second millenniums B.C. About the beginning of the second millennium, the great king of the Twelfth Dynasty was forced to take the most extensive measures to curb the northward thrust from Ethiopia. By building dozens of gigantic fortresses in Nubia, the Egyptians succeeded in curtailing for some three or four hundred years the Ethiopian expansion towards the north. With the collapse of the great Twelfth Dynasty, thought by some Egyptologists to have been brought about by Ethiopian pressure from the south, the movement reasserted itself only to be curbed again, first by the Hyksos invasion of Egypt and then by the powerful kings of the Eighteenth Dynasty.

The more the matter is investigated, the more it seems that the Erythryaean (Red) Sea was in ancient times a great highway connecting East Africa with Lower Mesopotamia and northern India. Old trade routes connecting Meroe with the Red Sea ports are known to have existed in Meroitic times, and no one knows how long before. This brings us to the crux of the matter with which we are concerned. The early Greek traditions record that the father of Memnon (King of the Ethiopians) was holding sway in Persia, or Susa, and that it was from this point that Memnon, with a consolidated army of Ethiopians and soldiers from India, marched to the succor of his kinsmen at Troy. What, then, if the old Ethiopian stock had succeeded in holding its own in part at least of the Persian area down to the time of the Trojan War, and what if the royal houses of Ethiopia, Susa, and Troy VI were related through intermarriage in a manner similar to what seems to have been the case in Ethiopia and Egypt?

Documentary evidence—the Amarna Letters*—testifies to the certainty of such relationships between the Asian kingdoms and ancient Egypt. Moreover, the Asian wives of both Amenhotep III and his son Amenhotep IV were princesses from kingdoms, Mitani and Babylon, that lay along the highway between Troy and Susa, so that it is not at all impossible that the kingdoms of these princesses were also connected by commercial ties and perhaps by kin with the kingdoms of both Troy and Persia. In addition, it is also quite possible that both Babylon and Mitani were directly connected by kinship with the royal families of Ethiopia. For it is true that both Amenhotep III and Amenhotep IV visited extensively and, indeed, lived much of their time in Ethiopia. Traces of what seems to have been a palace of Amenhotep III were found in Meroe. It is thus no great strain on logic to argue that some of the sons and daughters, or other relatives of the Asian wives of Amenhotep III and his son, might have married into the royal houses of Ethiopia, thus tying by blood the royal families of Mitani and Babylon, and perhaps also Troy and Persia with the royal families of Egypt and Ethiopia. Hence, to assert again, when ancient traditions make Memnon, king of Ethiopia; Tithonus, governor of Persia; and Priam, king of Troy to be kinsmen, it is entirely possible that we have a family connection which was not beyond historical possibility.

Scholars have long held that the Trojan War was caused by commercial rivalries between the Trojans and the Achaean Greeks, while others think it was occasioned by a united attempt of the Achaeans to plunder and acquire for themselves the old and wealthy cities of the Troad, Troy being only the

*These letters are the official correspondence of Amenhotep III and his son, Akhnaton. *Ed.*

most conspicuous. If these hypotheses are sound, it is only natural that Susa and the other kingdoms for which Troy was the chief port to the west should come to Troy's aid in such a threatening commercial situation. And if the Trojan royal family was connected by blood ties with these kingdoms, as ancient legend affirms in the cases of Susa and Ethiopia, we have an even stronger reason for the two latter kingdoms bestirring themselves in Troy's behalf.

A generation or so after Homer (the early eighth century B.C.), Greek poets in widely distant parts of the Greek world were referring to Ethiopia and Memnon with the same ease and readiness which characterized the Homeric usages. For example, Hesiod, who was a citizen of Boetia on mainland Greece, and whose sole experiences of the sea is said to have been a voyage of forty yards across the Euripus, made a passing allusion to Memnon, king of the Ethiopians, and employed a casual reference to the "dusky" inhabitants of the distant kingdom, a reference which would have had no meaning whatever to a people not already more or less familiar with facts or traditions concerning Ethiopia and its peoples. About the same time, Arctinus of Miletus in Asia Minor was penning the lengthy *Ethiopis*, which had as its principal theme the exploits at Troy of the Ethiopians and the death of Memnon, their king.

Now this wide geographical range of the Memnonian legend at so early a stage in the development of Greek tradition, together with its great popularity and even wider range in later times, makes it difficult to believe that that part of the stock traditions upon which it was based was not itself founded upon an actual historical occurrence. Indeed, the more one reflects upon the many references to Memnon, the more one inclines towards the view that the Greek poets may have had at their disposition written records dating from an earlier age which provided a documentary basis for their allusions to

Ethiopia's participation in the great Mycenaean conflict. Indeed, the possibility of the ancient existence of such a document or documents is, broadly speaking, not a new idea. Strabo strongly held that the *Iliad* and the *Odyssey* were based on earlier Phoenician records of travel, and V. Berard in his learned and ingenious book *Les Phéniciens et l' Odyssée* has propounded at quite some length a similar thesis.

The Phoenicians were a very old and much traveled people; Thucydides implied that they were cruising about in Aegean waters in Minoan times; Homer and Herodotus reported their presence in the eastern Mediterranean at the dawn of Greek history; and in the Old Testament their voyages on "Tarshish ships" and their visits to the "Land of Ophir" find frequent mention. The Phoenicians were, therefore, in all probability well informed on affairs in and about the Mediterranean basin and in neighboring lands in the second and first millenniums B.C. They must, perforce, have been thoroughly conversant with the facts and events pertaining to the great Trojan conflict. If, then, the opinions of Strabo and V. Berard are sound, Homer's allusions not only to Memnon but to other Ethiopian events and incidents could have been based on documentary sources. And if this was the case with the *Iliad* and the *Odyssey,* the same might equally have been true of Hesiod's allusion to Memnon in the *Theogony* and of Arctinus' commemoration of the celebrated Ethiopian in the *Ethiopis.* Hence, although there have been found no specific archeological remains attesting to the presence of Ethiopians at Troy, it is by no means improbable that they were, as ancient tradition affirms, really allied with the Trojans against the Achaeans in that most memorable of proto-historical conflicts.

For the better part of the eighth and the earlier half of the seventh centuries B.C., there is not much to say, but for the sixth century the evidence is fairly abundant and illuminating. It may be said at once that there has been discovered, on widely scattered Greek sites in and around the eastern end of the Mediterranean basin, a number of archeological remains which clearly indicate that the Greeks of the sixth and seventh centuries were evidently very closely acquainted with the Ethiopian type. Indeed, this evidence seems to prove that there was a relatively large Ethiopian population in the Greek world at this period. There are a relatively large number of ceramic remains showing black figures as decorative motifs and, in many instances, the ethnic traits of the type are so realistically portrayed that scholars are convinced that living models must have been employed.

Grace Hadley Beardsley in her interesting little book, *The Negro in Greek and Roman Civilization*, has listed the scattered notices of several hundred objects of the kind covering, as the title of her work indicates, the whole of the classical period. It is to her study that we are, in the main, indebted for the descriptive accounts of the specimens included in the following review. According to this source, there are now to be found in many of the leading museums of the world more than a score of these objects dating from the sixth and seventh centuries B.C. Among these fragments are three vases, now in the British Museum, which are catalogued as having come from the Greek colony of Naukratis in Egypt. On two of these, the features of the figures, though somewhat conventionalized, are nevertheless interpreted as portraying the Ethiopian type. On the other fragment, however, "the [Negro] type is strongly marked, the lips are prominent and everted, the nose short and broad and the hair woolly."

Attributed to Naukratis of the sixth century B.C. are also a small series of paste, glass, or steatite pendants for earrings or necklaces shaped in the likeness of Negro heads. Four of these are in the British Museum and one in the Bulak Museum at Cairo. From the North African Greek Province of Cyrenaica there has come to the Louvre a sixth century terra cotta figurine of an Ethiopian in which "the forehead is low and lips large." Excavations at Camirus on the island of Rhodes have yielded figurines of a very similar type; six of these are now in the possession of the British Museum. The neighboring island of Cyprus has sent to the Metropolitan Museum an object of the same general stamp. Coming from the same island are two janiform ointment vases of faience representing two distinct ethnic types; one of these, dating from the seventh century and now in the Antiquarium in Berlin, depicts a bearded "barbarian" head to which is conjoined "the head of a Negro with a smooth face. The latter has a broad flat nose and thick lips. His woolly hair is indicated by squares blocked out in the faience." The second vase, now in the British Museum, is quite similar, with the exception that the Ethiopian's hair instead of being blocked out as in the Berlin vase, is indicated by lozenge-shaped incisions with a dot in the center of each."

Cyprus, like Naukratis, has also yielded a small series of paste and steatite pendants modeled or carved to represent Negro heads. The Arndt Collection in Munich has two examples in which the artist has indicated the woolly hair by means of a series of raised dots; the Metropolitan Museum has one in which the hair is shown by a series of drilled holes and another where the curly hair is indicated by a lozenge-shaped incision similar to those on the janiform vase in the British Museum. From Cyprus, again, there has come to the British Museum "a thin strip of gold embossed with rosettes and conventionalized animal heads. In the center of the strip at the top is the mask of an Ethiopian on its side." The celebrated little island of Aegina has yielded a single "paste scarabaeus of Naucratite fabric with an Ethiopian head in high relief," which is now in Berlin. From Tyre there has come to the British Museum a scarabaeus of a somewhat similar type.

Mainland Greece of the sixth century B.C. is represented by

"a series of plastic vases in the form of heads, some single, some janiform—on these the racial types are rendered with great fidelity—here is the true Negro type, woolly-haired, prognathous, with broad nose and large everted lips." Beardsley observes, "There is no doubt that Ethiopians were actually on Greek soil and that they served as models for the potter."

In the Metropolitan Museum is a sixth century oenochoe from Athens in the form of a single Negro head. The following brief account of the famous Caeretan hydra, discovered at Caere in Etruria and now in Vienna, will provide a fitting conclusion to what we have to say on this head. On this celebrated vase are depicted scenes suggested by the myth of Hercules' encounter with Busiris, a legendary king of Egypt. Briefly, it may be recalled that the myth relates that a certain soothsayer, Phrasius of Cyprus, went to Egypt where he found a famine in the land. He told the king that the kingdom's woes could be put to an end only through the sacrifice of all foreigners to the gods, whereupon Busiris and his priest straightway seized the soothsayer and put him to death. Hercules, during one of his visits to Africa, fell into the hands of the officers of the king and was scheduled to meet the same fate, and the scenes of the Caeretan vase memorialize an incident in that event. According to the myth, Hercules permitted himself to be led to the altar without any show of resistance, but just as the rites were about to commence, he turned on Busiris and his priest and killed them with his club and his bare hands. On one side of the hydra is a spirited representation of this scene. The other side shows a group of Negroes or Ethiopians rushing to the aid of the prostrate priests and their king. The king and six of the priests are represented as having straight hair and brown skins; five priests, however, are black, though their hair is straight. The Ethiopians who are coming to the assistance of the priests and the king are thus: "Their hair is very woolly and their jaw structure prominent." The vase, though found in Italy, is believed by some authorities to have been imported from North Africa, probably Naukratis.

The foregoing citations are sufficient to show that the physical characteristics of the Ethiopian type were clearly well known to the Greeks of the seventh and sixth centuries B.C. And as Beardsley suggests, the portrayal of the features of the type are generally too lifelike to have been based upon word or memory pictures alone but must have been copied from living models. In short, there were evidently a goodly number of blacks actually living on Greek soil at this time.

This survey of Greek contacts with the African continent during ancient times reveals that there were several ways whereby black Africans may well have entered the Greek and Aegean communities. Beardsley has suggested that the Greek commercial colony at Naukratis in Egypt—founded, it is generally held, sometime in the early part of the sixth century B.C. —was perhaps the chief center through which Aegean peoples of this era established their contact and acquaintance with the Ethiopian type, and there is much to be said for this point of view. It is true that only a generation or two before Pharaoh Psammetichus had granted the Greeks the privilege of establishing themselves at Naukratis, all Egypt had been under Ethiopian control, and under such circumstances it is quite possible that Naukratis, like other Egyptian towns of the time, still had a large Ethiopian population. Peoples from almost every part of the Greek world seem to have congregated at Naukratis, for Herodotus tells us that in this African city there was a temple called the Hellenium which had been jointly built by the citizens of Chios, Teos, Phocaea, Clazomenae, Rhodes, Cindus, Halicarnassus, Phaselis, and Mytilene. "Three [Greek] nations, however, consecrated for themselves separate temples [at Naukratis], the Aeginetans one to Zeus, the Samians to Hera, the Milesians to Apollo."

Ethiopia (Auxum and Kush) was at this time a powerful

nation both commercially and politically; her diplomatic, cultural, and trading contacts with Egypt were very close; hence it is reasonable to assume that, in addition to the normal black population, there must also have been in this famous commercial entrepôt of Greek merchandise a large number of Ethiopian traders who had come to share the advantages offered by its cosmopolitan markets. It is quite possible that much of the enormous quantities of gold and ivory employed by the Greeks in building their great chryselephantine statues reached the Greek islands and the Greek mainland through such means; and it may be that it was from Naukratis, too, that came many of those Greek objects that archeologists like G. A. Reisner, D. R. MacIver, John Garstang, and other investigators have found in such large numbers in the tombs and temple ruins of Ethiopia. But however this may be, enough has been said to show that Naukratis was probably an important center for the meeting of Greeks and Ethiopians in the seventh and sixth centuries B.C., and in the light of these same considerations, we might venture to suggest that it was doubtless from this port that set sail some of those blacks whom Dr. Beardsley thinks served as models for Greek potters and artisans.

Naukratis, however, was not the only North African city where Greeks and black Africans of the pre-classical period may have come to know and treat with one another. About the same time that the Greeks were establishing themselves in this Egyptian city, some of their compatriots were engaged in similar enterprises on the African coast farther towards the west. Cyrene, located between the Syrtes and Egypt and founded about the middle of the seventh century B.C. by a colony of Dorians from Thera, is worthy of special mention in this connection. Cyrene itself became a flourishing metropolis and around it were grouped the four minor cities of Barce, Teucheira, Hesperedes and Appollinia, all of them colonies or offshoots of Cyrene itself. Indeed, some scholars hold that Ionic Greeks of the sixth century even invaded the Phoenician or Carthaginian sphere of influence and established colonies and trading posts along the Barbary Coast. The evidence for this is derived from surviving Ionic names of small towns and islands along the western portion of the North African coast.

Much like the North African cities and towns in later historic times, these proto-historic Greek settlements were, in all probability, northern terminals of trade routes stretching away towards the interior of Africa; and over these routes there doubtless came with their products blacks who might well have found their way eventually to the Greek lands in and about the eastern Mediterranean. Hence the suggestion that the Ethiopians represented on Greek pottery and other remains of the seventh and sixth centuries B.C. imply the presence of blacks on Greek soil at that date is not far-fetched. On the basis of the same kind of evidence, it has been shown that blacks, or Ethiopians, were apparently even more numerous in Greek lands in the fifth century B.C., for Beardsley's list for this century includes more than a hundred specific objects definitely representing the Ethiopian type, which, like those of the preceding centuries, are often so lifelike that they must have been based to a large extent upon living models. The fourth century is respresented by an equally large number of such objects, and it may also be pointed out that about this time figures of Ethiopians are known to have appeared for a while on the coinage of Athens and Delphi.

Obviously, the blacks represented on these wares dating from the seventh and sixth centuries were certainly known to the Greeks long before Xerxes' invasion of Greece, and unless we assume that many of the Africans who accompanied the Persian army in its march through the country settled down in Greece, it becomes difficult to believe that the black types shown on the objects dating from the fifth and fourth centuries could be attributed to that source. And again, since the Ptolemaic relationships with Ethiopia—regarded by some scholars as the original avenues of Greco-Ethiopian Acquaintanceship—were not established until a century or so later, it is of course impossible that the inspiration for the previously mentioned objects can be traced to that source.

The evidence summarized in this chapter seems to establish the conclusion that the relations between black, or Ethiopian, folk and the Greeks of the post-Homeric and early classical age, were, as in the pre-Homeric or Minoan and Mycenaean periods, more extensive and direct than the historians and classical scholars have been wont to think. It is needless to stress how the discoveries and studies which have contributed to these points of view have done much to tone down the skepticism previously entertained by scholars with respect to the historical value of the references and allusions to Ethiopia and the Ethiopians contained in the earlier of the classical works. The facts and considerations hitherto advanced touch this important question only in its broader and more general aspect. The following chapters are devoted to a more specific critical survey and appraisal of the historical value of the Ethiopian notices in the works of some of the more important Greek and Roman authors.

# III

## The Classical Sources: Poets and Playwrights

## Introduction

I f a complete roster should be compiled of all the classical authors who are known to have composed works containing notices of Ethiopia, such a list would include very close to a hundred names. The original works of many of these authors are now lost; but in many instances their contents, or parts of them, are known, and excerpts are preserved in classical works which are still extant. In the preceding chapter, it was pointed out that most of the classical writings mentioned in this connection can be divided into two general groups; first, those composed by poets, dramatists, and romancers, and treating mainly topics of a more or less legendary or mythological nature; and second, those written by historians, naturalists, and geographers, dealing for the most part with matters and events of an allegedly historical character.

No attempt will be made to compile and comment on all of the authors and works included in these two general groups. For our purposes such an effort is neither practical nor necessary. While passing mention is made of the names and works of most of the more important of these writers, the major purpose of this chapter is to attempt a critical review of some of the Ethiopian notices contained in the works of a small but representative number of these authors with the object of examining the value and import of such references to students of African history. In choosing the writers to be considered, two general guiding principles were maintained. The first was to select the authors in such a way that every major period of the classical age and each of the general literary groups named would be represented; and the second was to select, other things being equal, those authors whose works are most available and best known to the general public.

The concern of this chapter will be the poets and playwrights, Homer, Hesiod, Arctinus of Miletus, and Ovid.

## HOMER

The parentage and nationality of Homer—just where he was born and when, or indeed if he was ever born or ever lived at all—are questions which Homerists long have debated among themselves with much heat and zeal. According to an old document, dating in its present form from the time of the Emperor Hadrian but seemingly based in part on an older work composed about 400 B.C., we learn that seven cities, Smyrna, Rhodes, Colophon, Salamis, Chlios, Argos, and Athens, claimed the illustrious poet as a native son. Aristarchus, head of the great Alexandrian Library in the second century B.C., who was famed as one of the greatest of the ancient Homerists, favored Athens as Homer's birthplace.

This diversity of opinion among the ancients themselves concerning the personal history of their greatest poet contributed, no doubt, much towards the growth and development of that general skepticism which the Wolfian school a few generations ago was so earnestly expressing about things Homeric. There were among the scholars associated with this school some who not only rejected outright the historicity of the Homeric themes but who even went so far as to question whether such a man and poet as Homer had ever existed at all.

Archeological research, supplemented by reexaminations and new evaluations of the internal evidence in the Homeric poems themselves, together with statements about the poet in other ancient works, has, however, just about dissipated these older skeptical attitudes. While the cumulative results of such investigations have led scholars generally to take the position that Homer was a real person, there is still, as in ancient times, some divergency of opinion on just when he lived. Aristotle and Aristarchus thought that he flourished about 1044 B.C.; Herodotus, on the other hand, places him around 850 B.C. Though there are some notable exceptions, Homerists of our times seem, on the whole, to favor the latter date.

As Homerists are now generally inclined to accept the historicity of a personal Homer, so is there a growing tendency to credit him with having worked out in their basic forms the *Iliad* and the *Odyssey* that are inseparably connected with his name. We say that he is credited with having produced the *Iliad* and *Odyssey* in their basic forms, for it is generally admitted that both, as we have actually received them, in all probability vary somewhat from the original drafts. This was probably brought about by interpolations and other changes made by Pisistratus, Aristarchus, and later Homerists of ancient times in their editions of both works. These changes, however, are not thought to have materially affected the fundamental theme or themes of the works, which are now supposed to represent a fairly accurate account of actual episodes and events which occurred in the Aegean world several centuries before Homer's times. In other words, there is a growing disposition among modern scholars to conclude, as did Strabo, that "Homer's narrative is founded upon history."

Thus, although the poet did indeed often adorn and embellish actual occurrences by gilding them with the "beauties of fancy," it seems that he was seldom guilty of "inventing an empty fable apart from the inculcation of truth." It is now generally admitted that the accounts of many of the personages, places, and events related by Homer were, as Strabo said, "no mere inventions of poets or contemporary scribblers, but the records of real actors and scenes."

There were, however, among the Homerists of antiquity some few who were wont to add certain other reservations and qualifications regarding the historical and geographical subject matter preserved in Homer's works. Eratosthenes, for example, one of the leading students and critics of Homer in ancient times, enunciated the principle that, while the celebrated poet was well versed on geographical and historical matters relating to Greece and its immediate environs, he was nevertheless very poorly informed on, indeed quite ignorant of, similar facts appertaining to regions outside of the immediate Greek area. This view was adopted in varying degrees by several other eminent Homeric critics of the period, among them Aristarchus of Alexandria, Apollodorus, the grammarian, and Crates, the librarian at Pergamum. But Strabo, whose geographical knowledge was far ahead of that possessed by the critics named, while admitting that there was a modicum of truth in this view, showed that the criticism was by no means so well founded as Eratosthenes and others of the Alexandrian period believed. The growth of modern knowledge has had the effect of showing that Strabo's position was quite sound. Nowhere is the justice of Strabo's more liberal attitude towards the poet more effectively demonstrated than in modern research, which has tended to substantiate the general truth of many of Homer's statements concerning Ethiopia and the Ethiopians. Recent archeological explorations in Ethiopia, supplemented by the observations of ethnologists and other investigators, have shown that a number of the poet's allusions and references to the distant land and its peoples reflected a familiarity with Ethiopian conditions which could only have been based on an extremely close knowledge of the facts.

Before taking up this phase of our discussion, it may be well to consider briefly the possible sources from which Homer derived his information. Diodorus relates that during his stay in Egypt, certain Egyptian priests read to him a statement "out of their sacred book" to the effect that many of the "wise and learned men [the bards who preceded Homer and from whom he is said by some to have derived some of his themes] among the Grecians journeyed to Egypt in ancient times" and that it was through their efforts that many of the most distinguishing features of early Greek civilization were first transported from Egypt to Greece. In this connection, Diodorus remarks that he was specifically informed that among the most ancient of this group were Orpheus, who carried back to Greece the entire fable of hell, as well as many of the religious rites and ceremonies which later became well established in the land; Musaeus, whose specific borrowings from Egypt Diodorus does not give, although tradition makes him a disciple of Orpheus; Melampodes, who brought into Greece the rites and solemnities of Bacchus (Dionysus) and the fabulous story of Saturn and the Titans; Daedalus, whose knowledge of sculpture and architecture was considerably influenced by what he learned in Egypt; and Homer, the poet, who, during his sojourn in Egypt, learned from the Egyptians the facts concerning that medicine which caused human beings to forget their anger and sorrow and which, as Homer says, Helen gave to Telemachus in order that he might no longer remember his sadness of the past. It was also from Egypt, Diodorus records the Egyptian priests as affirming, that Homer "derived his story of the embraces between Jupiter and Juno and [the accounts of] the visits of the gods to Ethiopia."

While scholars who are inclined to believe in the existence of a personal Homer may be willing enough to admit that the poet was in all probability a widely traveled man, yet it must be confessed that aside from Diodorus' notation, there is no other known reference to this supposed visit to Egypt, and it may well be that the whole account of the poet's African sojourn, as well as that of his alleged predecessors, is a pure fabrication. On the other hand, it cannot be denied that there are certain independent considerations which would seem to indicate that there may be some basis in truth for the account; comparative studies of early Greek and Egyptian civilizations have revealed that there were some striking parallels between the specific art forms and the religious beliefs and practices referred to by Diodorus. Beliefs and ceremonies connected with the Egyptian worship of Osiris and Isis were startlingly like those fostered by the Greeks towards Bacchus (Dionysus) and Ceres; and the earliest of archaic Greek sculpture, that typified in the Nekandra statue, the Apollos of Thera, Melos, Orchomenos, and Delphi, and the seated figures from Branchedae, are fashioned on the same fundamental esthetic principle—the rule of the law of frontality which characterized Egyptian sculpture throughout its history. Moreover, as we shall soon specifically point out, certain independent literary sources and certain archeological discoveries and ethnological observations in Egypt and the Sudan have provided some striking evidence which seems to offer a very good explanation of the origin of the Homeric notion that the Olympian divinities paid a yearly visit to Ethiopia. Hence, it is not at all beyond the bounds of reasonable conjecture to assume that Diodorus' informants spoke the truth when they informed him that Homer and his predecessors had actually visited and learned much from Egypt. In this connection it may be well to note that modern archeological research has shown that, throughout the period in which these alleged visits may have occurred, a large Ethiopian population was dwelling in Egypt. (See Chapter II.)

In further consideration of the Homeric sources, it is to be noted that V. Berard in his learned and ingenious book *Les Phéniciens et l'Odyssée* sought to establish Strabo's contention that the *Odyssey* in particular was perhaps at least partly based on an old Phoenician corpus of sailing directions. Certain recent students of the subject admit the *Odyssey* is quite true to sea life, that it "smells of brine and seaweed and ozone," and that it was doubtless based on some old well-crystallized traditions of seamanship; but these scholars are inclined to think that the theory of the Phoenician origin for these is perhaps not as well founded as Berard's thesis would claim. If Homer did indeed have at his disposal a collection of mariners' experiences—and it is agreed that this is quite probable—the opinion is that these are to be credited not primarily to Phoenician but rather to older Aegean or Minoan sources.

Cumulative evidence seems to favor the latter view, for it is now generally agreed that the Homeric themes were to a large extent quite definitely based on Minoan rather than Phoenician activities and traditions, a thesis which is now much more soundly established than it was in 1902 when Berard first elaborated his ideas. Moreover, on the basis of the theory proposing an Aegean or Minoan background for the *Odyssey*, it is possible to bring forward certain specific bits of evidence which seem to explain the source, or sources, of Homer's references and allusions to Ethiopia and Ethiopians. There is now available a considerable mass of evidence which strongly indicates that there were definite and extensive communications between the Aegean area and blacks in Africa in the Minoan period. Thus, since the *Odyssey*, like the *Iliad*, allegedly embodies many traditions which go back to these times, it is quite reasonable to suppose that some of Homer's Ethiopian notices may, in all probability, be reflexes of these older contacts. With these comments in mind, we may now turn our attention to a consideration of some specific references made by the illustrious poet to Ethiopia and Ethiopians.

A consideration of the narrative and descriptive content of some Homeric passages in the light of modern archeology and anthropology provides evidence of a quality sufficient to warrant the assertion that Homer and his contemporaries knew their Ethiopia better than contemporary scholarly opinion, on the whole, has been wont to allow. To be sure, the location and description of the "Land of Black-faced men" are rather vague and limited, but that the poet-geographer knew the general direction in which the country lay, as well as something of its natural features annd external conditions, is clearly demonstrated in both the *Iliad* and the *Odyssey*.

In the *Iliad* the poet locates Ethiopia near the uttermost rim of the inhabited earth: "On the warm limits of the farthest main"; and in the *Odyssey* he, as did Herodotus centuries later, divides the people and the land into two parts, one towards the sunrise and the other toward the sunset, for the Ethiopians were "A race divided; whom the sloping rays/The rising and the setting sun surveys." The poet's meaning in these passages has provided Homerists with subject for prolonged and heated debate from the times of Aristarchus, Crates, and Strabo down to our own day. Some scholars, ancient and modern alike, have contended that Homer's "race divided" implies that he thought the Ethiopians were inhabitants of both Asia and Africa, while other scholars have asserted that the poet meant to refer only to the Ethiopians above (south of) Egypt as a divided race, the division being made by the Nile River. It is no easy matter to settle the contending claims of these two schools of thought, for much convincing evidence has been, and still can be, advanced on both sides. At first, the latter view may seem to be nearer the truth; but the ancients also maintained that there were Ethiopians in Asia. Strabo quotes the geographer Ephorus, whose works are now lost, as saying that it was "the opinion of the Ancients that the country of the Ethiopians extended from the rising to the setting sun and that Scythia was opposite it." References to the Ethiopians in the *Theogony* of Hesiod, in the fragments of Aeschylus' *Prometheus Bound*, and in the fragment of the *Phaethon* by Euripides have also been interpreted as implying that a similar tradition was current when these authors lived and wrote. And Herodotus also expressed the same general idea when he wrote abut contingents of Asian Ethiopians in the polyglot army of Xerxes.

Consequently, it is by no means easy to deny that a similar notion may have existed in Homer's day and that in speaking of the Ethiopians as being divided, the poet might have had in mind Ethiopians who were thought to have lived in Asia as well as in Africa. In this connection it may be well to remember that modern research has revealed that there was, as ancient opinion maintained, a significant Ethiopian population in western and southern Asia in ancient times. If Homer intended to reflect such a view, he was perhaps not very far from the truth, for recent archeological, anthropological, and historical inquiry has brought, and is bringing, to light evidence which supports the conclusion that Palestine, Arabia, Persia, and India were once the seats of important groups of blacks or Africans, and that the traces of this racial type, which are still to be detected in most of these areas at the present time, are but the surviving remnants, members of the once more firmly established ethnic group.

But whatever may have been Homer's belief and intent relative to Asian Ethiopians, there can be but little doubt that he intended the reference in question to include the Ethiopia and the Ethiopians of Africa. Strabo, while leaning to the view that Homer had in mind also Asian Ethiopians, is nevertheless convinced that he "alludes to the Ethiopia contiguous to Egypt," and he also thought that the poet meant to imply that it was the Nile that "divided Ethiopia into two parts." E. H. Bunbury, in his *History of Ancient Geography*, also observed that Homer's division of Ethiopia would appear to show that "the notion of the existence of black races in the east and the west of Africa had already reached the ears of the poet." M. Cary and E. H. Warmington in their book, *The Ancient Explorers,* adopted the view that the eastern section of Homer's Ethiopians "were the Negroes of the Somali coast— and that the western moiety were the Sudanese whose land stretched westward *ad infinitum* from the Nile Valley."

With respect to Homer's knowledge of Ethiopian geography, it may be pointed out that in the *Odyssey* he alluded to the Nile as "Egypt's heaven-descended stream"; and Diodorus quoted a passage from a poem attributed to Homer but otherwise unknown in which the poet specifically stated that the great river had its origin on a "... mountain high with pleasant woods adorn'd [Lake Tana?]."

It would seem from these two allusions, particularly the latter, that the poet possessed authentic knowledge concerning two of the major features of the Nile: first, that although Egypt had little rain, the waters of Egypt's Nile were pluvial, and not, as some of the later Greeks believed, the gift of a spring located near the first cataract; and second, that the sources of the river were situated, as indeed those of the Blue Nile are, in a mountainous region where trees or "pleasant woods" abounded.

More striking still as an instance of the accuracy of Homer's knowledge concerning Ethiopia and its peoples is that celebrated passage in which he alluded to the yearly visits paid by the cranes to the land of the "dwarfs." The substance of the story, as Homer epitomized it, was that on the distant boundaries of Ethiopia there dwelt a diminutive people to whom the cranes were deadly enemies, for on the approach of winter in the northern climes the cranes were said to "Take wing, and over the ocean speed away" to the southern lands, bearing "fearful blood-shed and death to the small Pygmaean race." Although Homer, as far as our present records reveal, was the first to refer to these little African people, he was by no means the only ancient writer who is known to have mentioned them. In the *Catalogue of Women* there is a statement which definitely implies that Hesiod alluded to the Pygmies in one of his lost works, and in the surviving fragments of Hecataeus, the celebrated Milesian geographer, there is a most interesting account of this "dwarf-like" race who are said to have been an agricultural people. And in Herodotus' day the tradition was current that a black-complexioned and "dwarfish" race dwelt in the inner regions of Africa. Aristotle also spoke of a similar people living beyond the marshy districts about the Upper Nile; and Pomponius Mela referred to these little people and spoke of them as fighting with cranes.

Notwithstanding these numerous ancient references, Homer's allusions to the Pygmies, as well as the later statements, were in the earlier days of modern geography regarded as notions with no foundation in fact. "The Pygmaean race," like the "Indian Dactyls" and other impish creatures, were dismissed as imaginary inhabitants of an ancient fairy world. However, the African travels of Du Chaillu, Livingston, Schweinfurth, and later explorers vindicated the ancients on this score, and the "dusky race" to whom they referred has been demonstrated as a reality. Moreover, on the strength of Egyptian evidence dating from the Old Empire, it seems certain that in ancient times the Pygmies of Africa lived much further north than they do at the present day, and hence may well have been known to Homer's informants.

Regarding Homer's allusion to the migration of the cranes from northern lands to the tropic climes, observations in natural history have fully established such alleged occurrences as actual fact. A Danish naturalist, Skovgaard, placed rings with his name engraved on them on the necks of some cranes, or white storks, and freed them in Schleswig, Denmark. Some time later, two of these, with the rings still in place, were found dead near Khartoum in the former Anglo-Egyptian Sudan. The announcement of this fact stimulated among the government officials of the ex-colony considerable interest in the migration of cranes, or white storks, from northern Europe to the Sudan, with the result that no little information has since been published on the matter. The outcome is that several observers have recorded the migration of thousands of cranes to and from the country.

From the foregoing considerations, we may reasonably conclude that Homer's allusions to the presence of Pygmies and migrating cranes in the southern land were not without foundation in fact, and that it is not improbable that the references reflect what was popular knowledge or a widely known tradition in the land of the poet's time. On this very point, Bunbury observes: "It is evident that the tradition here alluded to is one that the poet assumes to be familiar to all."

A further indication of the detailed character and the authenticity of Homer's knowledge concerning affairs in Ethiopia is reflected in the poet's allusions to certain of the religious practices carried on there. A notable instance of this is the passage in the *Odyssey* where the poet referred to an Ethiopian religious festival in which a "hecatomb", or sacrifice of bulls and rams, played an important part. Recent archeological research, supplemented by studies of cultural ethnologists, has revealed that the sacrifice of bulls and rams at religious ceremonies was not only a common and well established practice among the ancient Ethiopians but survived down to the present day as an important feature in the religious rituals practiced by modern descendants of the old Ethiopian people. In connection with these observations on the Ethiopian religious festivals, it may also be recalled that Homeric traditions frequently associated the great Olympian divinities with these ceremonies. In the first book of the *Odyssey*, the poet related that on the occasion of the council of divinities held in the interest of the long-suffering Odysseans, the god Poseidon was absent, being at the time "with the far-off Ethiopians" in order to share with them a "sacrifice of bulls and rams" in his honor. Again, when Iris, the goddess of the rainbow, went as messenger to Boreas and the "fierce-breathing Zephyrus" to invoke their aid in the funeral rites of "brave Patroclus," she was invited by the denizens of the winds to join them in a feast they were then celebrating. Iris, however, refused the invitation saying,

*Not now; for I again must take my way*
*Over the Ocean currents to the land*
*Where dwell the Ethiopians, who adore*
*The gods with hecatombs, to take my share*
*Of sacrifice.*

And yet again when Thetis promised her offended son Achilles that she would implore the aid of the gods in granting him revenge against the unfair Agamemnon, she warned him that he must be patient until the divinities return to Olympus from their yearly feast with the Ethiopians, for at that moment

*The sire of the gods and all the ethereal train*
*were then mixing with mortals and dining with*
*grace at the feast of Ethiopia's blameless race.*

In the opinion of some scholars, when Homer made Ethiopia into a kind of glorified campground and elevated "Ethiopia's blameless race" to a social position that made its members fit comrades for the gods, he not only committed a grave social indiscretion but indulged himself in poetic extravagance which is entirely without value to the student of history. A reconsideration of these passages in the light of later historical research brings to the fore certain facts which seem indeed to be of much significance. In the first place, it may be pointed out that Diodorus related that he was informed by the Egyptian priests that Homer's stories concerning the visits of the Olympian divinities to Ethiopia were based upon certain religious practices with which the poet doubtless became acquainted during his sojourn in Egypt. Among these, according to Diodorus, was a custom whereby the Egyptians once each year carried the tabernacles of certain of their great gods to Ethiopia and, after certain celebrations there, brought the shrines back to Egypt—"as if the gods had returned out of Ethiopia."

A passage in Procopius also informs us that it was an ancient custom of the Ethiopians living just to the south of Egypt to make a yearly pilgrimage to Philae, and after paying obedience to the goddess Isis, they would take her image into their country and some days later return it to its shrine on the sacred island. Unfortunately, neither of these notices specifies the number of days that the images of Egyptian divinities remained in Ethiopia, but it is safe to assume that the time connected with these ceremonies must have required several days, and it is interesting to note that Homer, in one of his allusions, specifically stated that:

> Twelve days the powers indulged the genial rite
> Returning with the twelfth revolving light.

I may mention yet another fact which is quite suggestive in connection with the whole question of the alleged visits of the Olympian divinities to Ethiopia. I refer to the interesting discovery of the distinguished German archeologist Karl Richard Lepsius. In the course of his far-reaching explorations in Ethiopia, he found on the walls of an old Ethiopian temple at Nagaa the outlines of a figure seemingly intended as a representation of the god Jupiter (Zeus) or Jupiter Seaphis. Although the god wears a triple crown composed of horns of the ram-god of the Ethiopians, the head of the figure is not only distinctly non-Negroid but remarkably Greeklike in cast, the face and beard recalling nothing quite so much as the surviving likenesses of the Phidian Zeus. In this same general connection, attention may again be called to Diodorus' remark that the Egyptian priest informed him that it was from Egypt that Homer derived his story of the embraces between Zeus and Hera.

Comparative studies of the religions of Ethiopia, Egypt, and Greece have revealed, as ancient traditions affirmed, that many of the gods of the countries were much alike in their fundamental attributes, that the Ethiopian forms of these gods were probably the oldest and very likely furnished the prototypes for those of Egypt and, ultimately by way of Egypt, the prototypes for those of Greece; and when it is recalled that ancient traditions were at one in making both the Egyptian gods and their Olympian counterparts pay yearly visits to Ethiopia, is it not possible to believe that Diodorus' Egyptian informants stated what was basically a fact when they said that the Greek gods themselves as well as Homer's accounts of their annual sojourn to "Ethiopia's happy climes" were derived from Egypt? If there is any virtue in the foregoing observations and suggestions—and it seems difficult to deny that there is some—then it follows that Homer's accounts concerning the visits of the Olympian divinities to Ethiopia are not without value to the historian.

One should also take note of those passages which seem to reflect the exceptionally high regard maintained by the ancient Aegean peoples towards their Ethiopian contemporaries. In this connection, it may be said that never before nor since have any peoples enjoyed the distinction of occupying such an exalted place in the literature of a foreign and unallied folk, and nowhere else in the annals of mankind are there to be found higher tributes to the character, honor, and valor of the blacks. In witness of Homeric sentiments in these respects, we have just seen that it was in "Ethiopia's happy climes" amidst "Ethiopia's blameless race," that popular and poetic tradition placed one of the most favored and most frequented retreats of the gods. Further high regard for the dusky-hued sons of the land is clearly reflected in those passages in which the imcomparable bard elevated certain individual members of the race to the position of veritable paragons of virtue and valor, even when judged by the standards applied in appraising the noblest of heroes in that valiant age. For example, the poet placed Memnon, king of the Ethiopians,* among the noblest of the nobles when he wrote:

> To Troy no hero came of nobler line
> Or if of nobler, Memnon it was thine.

And again in characterizing the black-skinned and frizzly-haired Eurybates, who was at once both the herald and the most favored companion of Odysseus, Homer likened him in depth of thought and breadth of soul to the great wanderer himself. For it was in Eurybates' "large soul alone Odysseus viewed an image of his own."

To be sure, it was once quite fashionable in academic circles to look upon Homer's characterization of the Ethiopians as a "blameless race" as well as the glowing tributes paid to Memnon and Eurybates as being entirely outside serious historical interest. Such references and allusions, it was held, were but graceful fictions and had no semblance whatever to

---

*Homer does not specifically say that Memnon was king of the Ethiopians, but Hesiod in the *Theogony* and Arctinus of Miletus in the *Ethiopis* and most writers of the classical period name him as Ethiopian king—Ed.

anything which even vaguely approached historical truth. But in view of the fact that many later classical writers, who drew their information from informants who had the opportunity of observing the Ethiopians at close range, repeatedly referred to their justice and magnanimity, it would seem that there was some real basis for those old and widespread traditions about the Aethiops. As we shall see, Herodotus, Diodorus, Callisthenes, and Heliodorus give particular prominence to this aspect of Ethiopian character. As for the historicity of those models of virtue and valor, Memnon and Eurybates, it may be said that later developments in archeology, ethnology, and ethnography, as they touch the countries and periods with which we are concerned, have revealed that it is entirely possible to believe that these two celebrated characters once walked the earth and indeed may well have performed the very parts accredited to them in Homer's immortal lines. For long before and long after the Trojan War, men of the type of Eurybates are known to have been domiciled in the Aegean; and the Ethiopians and Ethiopia of the age to which Memnon is assigned were quite capable of sending forth to foreign battle (indeed did send) legions and leaders which were quite as valiant as earlier traditions maintained.

The story of Memnon was one of the most widely circulated traditions of a non-Hellenic hero in the ancient world. In addition to the allusions to this prince in the works of Homer, passing references are also made to him by Hesiod, Arctinus of Miletus, Virgil, Ovid, Diodorus Siculus, Pausanias, and several other writers. Arctinus indeed composed a long poem in which Memnon is made the central hero; Diodorus said that "Memnon led to Troy 20,000 soldiers and 200 chariots and signalized his valor and reputation, with the death and destruction of many of the Greeks, till at length he was slain by an ambuscade lain for him by the Thessalineans."

Such then is the content and historical background of the

principal notices concerning Ethiopia which are to be found in the works of a most celebrated poet. When it is remembered that these references and allusions to Ethiopia and the Ethiopians were penned hundreds of years before any of the states or nations or civilizations of ancient European history were founded; and when there is no mention whatever in either the *Iliad* or the *Odyssey* to such ancient kingdoms or countries as Babylonia or Assyria, or Persia or India; and when it is remembered that Ethiopia occupies a more prominent place in the Homeric poems than does Egypt; and finally, when it is recalled that the Ethiopians were more frequently mentioned by the great poet than were his own kindred tribesmen, the Dorians and Hellenes themselves—these considerations together with those given in the preceding paragraphs make it clear that no student bent upon determining the real position of Ethiopia in world history can afford to ignore the gleams of light shed upon the subject by the greatest luminary of world literature, Homer.

Of course, some of the previously cited references and allusions have been richly embellished by the fertile bardic imagination; but the contention that these were simple fiction and hence of no value to the historian must be firmly disallowed. It seems safe to assume that these references and allusions were not only founded upon fact but were to a large extent reflexes of older and more widespread historic traditions whose details were already quite well known to the Aegean peoples of that age.

## HESIOD

**H**esiod, to whom we now turn our attention, has been chosen for consideration as much for his ancestral connections, and for the time and place in which he lived, as for the number and nature of his notices of

Ethiopia and Ethiopians. For although his known allusions to this land and its peoples are few and far between, yet when his early date and his provincial background are taken into account, the fact that he mentions Ethiopia at all becomes a matter of considerable historical significance. Hesiod, ranked by the ancients as second only to Homer, was, according to his own words, the son of a seafaring trader of Aeolis in Asia Minor. Pressed by poverty, the father of the poet forsook his native country and established himself as a farmer in continental Greece. There in a wretched hamlet, Ascra, which Hesiod himself describes as being "bad in winter, sultry in summer and good at no time," the future poet seems to have spent his youthful days either at work on his father's farm or in tending sheep.

Some scholars have not only treated these autobiographical notes as spurious but also doubted that such a man as the traditional Hesiod ever lived at all. On the other hand, there are critics who are inclined to accept these notices and who believe that the poet flourished sometime towards the end of the ninth or the beginning of the eighth century B.C. The arguments and conclusions of this later group seem to be convincing enough, especially since archeological research confirms that there is more truth in ancient records and traditions than was formerly supposed.

Turning now to Hesiod's notices of Ethiopia and the Ethiopians, it may be said that his references and allusions in this respect are not nearly so numerous or illuminating as those found in the work of Homer. In the *Theogony* he mentions in passing "brazen-crested [brass-helmeted] Memnon, king of the Ethiopians" and in *Works and Days* he casually alludes to "a land and city in the warm amd sunny south" whose inhabitants are "dark-faced men," a passage which, by reason of its general setting and content, is usually interpreted as referring directly to a city and a people of Ethiopia. While these are the only two notices of the Ethiopians found in the extant poems generally credited to Hesiod, there are nevertheless a number of references in the *Catalogue of Women*, a work dating to the same age as Hesiod and which seems to imply that in some of his lost compositions he frequently alluded to peoples, things, and events of the country in question.

One of these passages says: "let no one mock at Hesiod who mentions—the Troglodytes [a designation applied by the Greeks to people of Ethiopia] and the Pygmies," and another notes: "no one would accuse Hesiod of ignorance though he speaks of the Great Headed people and the Pygmies." Another closely associated fragment of the same work, whose context is not complete and whose meaning is not entirely clear but which was probably inspired by a Hesiodic remark, refers to "the Ethiopians, the Ligurians and the mare-milking Scythians." Attention should also be directed to Strabo who alluded to a mention of Pygmies by Hesiod.

Although these are the only references to Ethiopians which we can directly or indirectly trace back to Hesiod, they are, notwithstanding their briefness, incompleteness, and scarcity, quite significant when viewed in their general historical import. They would seem to indicate that by the end of the ninth or the beginning of the eighth century B.C. traditions about Ethiopians must have been quite well established even in the provincial and backward areas of the Greek world. That Hesiod, whose main vocation, it may be assumed, was that of a farmer and a shepherd, could have known anything at all of Ethiopia is itself a significant fact. But when it is remembered that his references, as is the case with those in Homer, are passing allusions with no attempt to explain them, it must be assumed that he took for granted that his hearers would understand what he meant.

Stories about the Ethiopian king, Memnon, the Troglodytes, the Pygmies, and the sunny cities of the black-faced

men must have been a part of the stock traditions of the Boeo-
tian peasantry at that time. Hence the aforementioned notices
of Hesiod, as well as those taken from the *Illiad* and the *Odyssey*, appear to point to the interesting conclusion that the fame
of Ethiopia had spread beyond the boundaries of Africa and
had become a part of the general knowlege of the greater
Aegean area centuries before most of the civilizations traditionally associated with antiquity had become known in this
part of the world. Hesiod, like Homer, makes no mention
whatever of Greece as such, or of Carthage, or of the then
powerful non-Hellenic nations of the ancient East; indeed, to
Egypt he only alludes in a passing reference to the Nile. Considerations such as these are most assuredly worthy of being
taken into account in any attempts to assign Ethiopia to her
rightful place in the outlines of world history.

## ARCTINUS AND OVID

A lthough Homer and Hesiod have been selected to
represent the ancient bards whose notices of Ethiopia are of special value to the student of Ethiopian history, our choice in this respect is not to be interpreted as indicating that they are necessarily the most important
of the poets who might have been chosen, Particularly is this
true of Hesiod; for there are two other poets whowell might
have been chosen in his stead. The first of these is the Ionian
bard, Arctinus of Miletus who, according to ancient traditions,
was one of the earliest, the best known, and the best loved
singers of antiquity. From the information now available, he
seems to have flourished about the time of the first Olympiad
(776 B.C.), and he is credited with having composed two poems,
the *Ethiopis* and the *Sack of Troy*, which taken together were
9,500 lines long. The purpose of these poems was to finish the

tale of Troy, which, so far as events were concerned, had been
left half told by Homer, who stopped his account with the
death of Hector. Both of these poems are now lost, but from a
digest of them preserved in the *Chrestomathea* of Proclus, who
is thought to have lived about the middle of the second century A.D., it appears that the *Ethiopis* was the story of the heroic
exploits and death of Memnon, king of the Ethiopians at the
siege of Troy. In this particular poem we have additional
evidence of the popularity and very wide range attained by
Ethiopian traditions in the Aegean world as early as the
eighth century B.C.

The second of the poets which should indeed be included
is Ovid, who in that remarkably brilliant work, *The Metamorphoses*, has preserved a number of most interesting notions
held by the ancient Greeks concerning Ethiopia, its history,
and its people. Notable among these are, first, his celebrated
account of the early Greeks' attempt to explain the origin of
the black skin color of the Ethiopians; second, his version of
the death and apotheosis of the Ethiopian King Memnon and
his long and detailed story of the events and developments
which eventuated in the marriage of Perseus to Andromeda,
the daughter of Cephus and Cassiopea, a king and queen of
Ethiopia.

When it is remembered that each of these poets, with the
exception of Ovid, lived and wrote in the very dawn of European literature at a time long before the "Golden Age" of
Ethiopian history, seventh to first century B.C., it can hardly be
denied that Ethiopia must have been a very ancient and yet
very virile force in order to have so firmly impressed itself on
the consciousness and memory of peoples so far removed
from the heart of Africa's sunny climes. Embedded in the *debris* of this traditional renown are many grains of golden truth
which the historian should use as substance and clues to different data and interpretations.

**G**reek drama as a poetic form reached its highest development in those incomparably stirring tragedies composed by Aeschylus, Sophocles, and Euripides, who flourished in Attica in the sixth and fifth centuries B.C. The sources of the life and inspiration of Greek drama went further afield than Attica, and had already been in existence hundreds of years before Aeschylus and Sophocles and Euripides were born. Like the Homeric and the cyclic poems which preceded them, the themes of the great Greek plays were founded, in the main, on events and episodes dating back to the age of the Trojan War and before. Furthermore, these themes had been for untold generations widely held traditions throughout the Aegean world. Moreover, the groundwork of the Greek drama as a poetic form was itself also very old, for the productions of Aeschylus and his successors represented the evolution and elaboration of an old folk festival carried out by the primitive Hellenic peoples each year in honor of Dionysus (or Bacchus), the god of wine.

As we have already seen, there is much archeological evidence and many ancient traditions which link Ethiopia and its African environs with the world of the heroes reflected in the Homeric and the later poems, and since the sources of the traditions used by the poets were essentially the same as those which were utilized by the dramatists, it is not surprising that the works of Aeschylus, Sophocles, and Euripides contained occasional notices of Ethiopia and the Ethiopians. It will, however, be somewhat surprising when we say that there are certain indications that the Dionysian festival which provided the foundations of the Greek drama may have had its origin in the inner or Ethiopian areas of Africa. We may take a brief pause to consider the traditions and the evidence which have prompted this suggestion.

Attention is called to Diodorus' assertion that the Egyptians held that Dionysus of the Greeks was the same as the Egyptian god Osiris, and that his worship was introduced into Greece in pre-Homeric times by Orpheus, Musaeus, and Melampodes after they had visited Egypt. Although it is impossible to verify the truth of this specific tradition, it is nevertheless true that comparative studies in Greek and Egyptian religions reveal that the older rites and worship associated with the god were remarkably alike in the two lands. In late Greek traditions Dionysus was looked upon as a son of Zeus and Semele and was said to have been born in Greece, but Diodorus informs us that ancient traditions affirmed that there were several gods by this name, and he cites the Egyptians and the Libyans as saying that the son of Zeus and Semele was one of the youngest and most recent of the number.

The original Dionysus, according to the Libyan tradition recorded by Diodorus, was the illegitimate son of Ammon, the king of a kingdom in inner Africa. Ammon, fearing the jealousy of his wife Rhea, concealed from her the birth of this son and secretly sent him away to the city of Nysa, which was in a country surrounded by a river and hence resembled an island. The legend gives the name of the all-embracing river as Triton, but since this was a kind of generic term applied to many rivers in early Greek geography, the name is of little assistance in identifying the area. There are, however, several other considerations which help in attempting to determine the probable region to which the legend refers. For while it is true that there are a number of ancient legends ascribing the name Nysa to places in many different parts of the world —Greece, Libya, Arabia, Babylonia, India, Egypt, and Ethiopia—it is also true that most of the older legends locate the Nysa associated with Dionysus in or near Ethiopia. Diodorus records that the Egyptians said that Dionysus was brought up at Nysa, a town in Arabia near Egypt. Herodotus has two passages of the same import. In one he specifically states that tradition affirmed that Dionysus was "carried off to Nysa, above Egypt in Ethiopia"; and in the other he refers to "the long-lived Ethiopians who dwell about the sacred city of Nysa and have festivals in honor of Bacchus [Dionysus]."

In addition, the description of this island as preserved in the Libyan traditions recalls at once what must have been in very ancient times the natural conditions of that African region surrounded by the Nile and its tributaries, the Atbara and the Blue Nile, and which was the heart of old Ethiopia, known to classical geographers as "Island of Meroe." Diodorus quotes an ancient poet who located "the sacred Nysa" where Dionysus was reared as being in the region "Where the streams of Egypt's Nile begins."

Dionysus, so tradition holds, first invaded Egypt and after installing as king Jupiter (Zeus), the youthful son of Rhea and Saturn, taught the Egyptians "the manner of planting, the use of the vine and how to keep and store up wine, and other fruits." Following this, Dionysus made a world tour, going as far as India; he taught the people there his improved arts of husbandry and agriculture and by these acts obliged all mankind to render him grateful remembrance and immortal honor.

Such then is some of the alleged African background of Dionysus, whose festivals gave rise to ceremonies which ultimately eventuated in the Greek drama. The Egyptians held, according to Diodorus, that the festivals and the rituals and ceremonies associated with them were introduced into Greece from Egypt by the pre-Homeric bards Orpheus and Musaeus. At the original festival to the Greek Dionysus, a part of the celebration consisted, according to Diodorus, "of a company of women once virgins who carried javelins decked with flowers and who ran about like furies hallooing and setting forth the praises of the god—as if he were then present among them."

As time passed these choruses became more refined and, in order to recall more widely the acts of the god, it has been supposed that other singers were added to mimic or enact some of the experiences which Dionysus and his companions were said by the traditions to have undergone. Thus it was, some authorities think, that the first stages of the drama were developed. Later still, further refinements were added and the action was extended to include not only experiences directly connected with Dionysus and his companions but other gods and heroes mentioned in the ancient traditions. These developments eventually culminated in the catholic plays of Aeschylus, Sophocles, and Euripides, in which the heroic sagas provided the themes and in which Dionysus (except in the *Bacchantes* of Euripides) seldom if ever appeared. But even in the golden age of Greek drama, when Dionysus was no longer an integral part of the play itself, his ancient connection with the drama as an institution was still symbolized by generally having present in or near the theatre a statue of the god; and he was always looked upon as the patron divinity of this form of art.

Of the 70 tragedies ascribed to Aeschylus only 7 have survived; of the 113 credited to Sophocles, again only 7 remain; and of the 92 dramas, including 8 satires, that are said to have been composed by Euripides, only 17 are left. Unfortunately for us, it turns out that those very dramas whose themes were such as to involve references to Ethiopia and the Ethiopians are all numbered among those that have been lost. For example, Sophocles and Euripides are each known to have written a drama entitled *Andromeda*, but neither of them now remains. It is safe, however, to assume that these were built, as the titles indicate, around the experiences of the Ethiopian princess Andromeda, the beloved daughter of Cephus, legendary king of Ethiopia, and his presumptuous queen Cassiopia.

A further hint of the popularity of Ethiopia with the

Greek dramatists as well as some idea of the nature and extent of their knowledge concerning the ancient land and its traditions may be inferred from the fact that they, as in the preceding instances, not only made Ethiopians the central figures of some of their plays but also included incidental references to the blacks and their country in certain other known works which were essentially European in theme and setting. Aeschylus, for example, in that immortal work *Prometheus Bound*, causes the long-suffering Titan to say to the unfortunate far-wandering Io that while she must avoid the "ford of Pluto" the Kisthene's Gorgonian plains "where dwell the gray-haired virgin Phorkedes," she may approach with safety the "tribes of black men" who dwell "by the Sun's fountain [near] Ethiopia's stream."

There are several other instances in which references and allusions are made to peoples and places in Africa which suggest certain Ethiopian connections or relationships. There are also certain quotations taken from some of the lost Greek dramas and preserved in extant works of other classical authors which relate specifically to Ethiopia and the Ethiopians. The following references are some notable instances that may be mentioned in this connection. Aeschylus, in *Prometheus Bound*, mentions Epaphos, who is described as "swarthy of hue," and of whom it is prophesied that "in the generation fifth from him" some of his descendants would leave their African home and establish themselves at Argos (in Greece), and that from one of this number there would spring a great Argive king "famed for his arrows."

A brief passage from an Aeschylian missing drama preserved in the pages of Strabo's *Geography* refers to "the sacred flood of the Red Sea with its bed of scarlet sands" near which was situated "a luxuriant marsh providing a plenteous food supply for the Ethiopians." In this connection, it may be pointed out that Strabo has also preserved a quotation from

Euripides's lost play, the *Phaethon*, in which there is a reference thought to be a passing allusion to the Ethiopians. From
this passage we learn that Clymene, the mother of Prometheus and Phaethon, was given to Merops, the sovereign of
some eastern kingdom within whose confines dwelt a race of
"swarthy men." Strabo interpreted this as being an allusion to
some distant Ethiopian nation situated on the shore of the
southern, or Erythraean (Red), Sea.

A further indication of the range and accuracy of early
Greek knowledge concerning Ethiopia is found in still
another passage attributed to Euripides. This too comes from
one of the lost plays and has survived through a quotation
preserved in the pages of Diodorus. In the section in question
the celebrated historian is summarizing the various conflict-
ing explanations advanced by the ancients for the overflow of
the Nile. Among the several opinions cited, he states that the
famous philosopher Anaxagoras ascribed the phenomenon of
the melting of the snows in Ethiopia, and that Euripides, who
was a pupil of the philosopher, concurred in this opinion, as
is witnessed in a passage in one of his plays (the name is not
given):

> The pleasant streams of th' river Nile forsakes,
> Which flowing from the Negro's parched land,
> Swells big when th' melting snow to th' river takes
> Comes falling down, and overflows the strand.

To appreciate the full significance of this passage it is
necessary to know that while the view it expresses is accepted
today without question, this was generally not the case among
some of the most noted ancient writers. It was not until about
the third century B.C. that this simple explanation received
much acceptance, and, indeed, as late as the first century B.C.
there were some noted students of the phenomenon—among
them Diodorus himself—who rejected the theory that the
melting snows of the Ethiopian or inner African mountains

were a factor in the process. Here then we seem to have a vital piece of evidence which appears to indicate that Anaxagoras and Euripides in the fifth century B.C. were better informed on certain aspects of inner African geography then were some writers of much later times.

The results of the preceding discussions, not withstanding the scarcity and often fragmentary character of the passages upon which they are based, would seem to justify the conclusion that the interest and knowledge of the Greek dramatists concerning Ethiopia and its peoples were by no means inconsequential or unconnected to the thoughts and traditions of the times. These are considerations which no student interested in a complete story of antiquity can with impunity afford to ignore.

# IV

## The Classical Sources: Historians and Geographers

## Hecataeus, Hellanicus, and Herodotus

C lassical literature in the earlier periods of its history was confined almost exclusively to poetic forms; until about 450 B.C. there were only the barest rudiments of prose. Indeed classical, or Greek, poetry had matured its last great form in the Attic drama before a true prose literature had begun. The origin of literary prose is thought to have been delayed in part by the paramount interest which epic poetry so long secured for the legends of the heroic past, and by the success with which elegiac or iambic verse subsequently responded to all the needs of expression felt by the cultivated and thoughtful Greeks in the earlier days of their history. The distinctive character of the small Greek states, together with the lack of any force making for a strong sense of national or racial unity, was likewise partially responsible for the delayed development of any common feeling or need of such unified traditions as might have stimulated a unified use of prose. It has been said that it was the pall cast by the Persian wars that inspired Greeks, as a whole, with their first genuine consciousness of a common kinship and supplied them with experiences which they came to feel could not be adequately memorialized in artistic forms. Following this awakening there sprang up alongside of that group of literary craftsmen known as the *epopoli,* or "narrators in verse," another group of writers designated as *logographi,* or "narrators in prose." The earlier writers belonging to this latter group soon came to be divided into two classes; first, those who concerned themselves mainly with speculative theology and the genealogies of gods and men; and second, those who interested themselves in the geography and history of their own and foreign lands.

It is an interesting and significant fact that just as the earliest of the *epopoli* included many references and allusions to Ethiopia in their poems, so did many of the earliest and greatest of the geographically and historically minded *logographi* find the ancient land and its inhabitants worthy of prominent mention in their prose narrations.

Hecataeus of Miletus, who flourished about the beginning of the fifth century B.C. and who earned for himself the appellation "Father of Geography" by writing the first systematic treatise on subjects in this field, is known to have included Ethiopia within the range of his studies and investigations. How extensive was his knowledge of the subject is not very clear, since his work, sometimes designated as the *Periodos* (General Survey) or sometimes by the more expressive title, *Tour of the Earth*, has long since been lost. Fragments and citations from this study have survived, however, in the writings of later classical authors, the most important collection of these being that preserved in the epitome of the *Ethnica* by Stephanus of Byzantium, who flourished in the time of Justinian I. Here Hecataeus is represented as referring specifically to at least two more or less distinct groups of peoples living in the general Ethiopian area. One of these groups was the Pygmies, who were said to have been an agricultural people.

That the original work contained a more extended account of the ancient land is very likely, for Hecataeus spent some considerable time in Egypt, having traveled up the Nile as far as Thebes where he conversed with the Egyptian priests, as did Herodotus after him. Stephanus cites the names of fifteen Egyptian cities taken from Hecataeus' lists, and Parhyrius tells us that many of the notices of the customs and manners of the ancient Egyptians found in the works of later writers were copied literally from the Milesian's account. Now when it is recalled that Hecataeus' sojourn in Egypt occurred only a few generations following the period when Egypt had been a colony of Ethiopia, and when it is remembered that Ethiopia was itself at this very period a land of great cities and flourishing culture, it is hardly to be doubted that much information concerning the southern land was available to him, nor is it to be supposed that he neglected to include this in his *General Survey.*

What Hecataeus essayed to do in the field of geography, another Ionian Greek, Hellanicus of Mitylene, who lived about 450 B.C., endeavored to do in history, for he is credited with having made the first systematic attempt to tell the story of Greece and its neighbors in Greek prose. The work is now lost but the tradition survives that he included in his survey not only accounts of the Greek states themselves but also discourses on Persia, Phoenicia, and Egypt as well. No mention is made in surviving notices of any specific references to Ethiopia, but since so many of the Greek writers who preceded him are known to have devoted considerable attention to that ancient land, it is hardly likely that he could have treated of Egypt without including something concerning Egypt's celebrated southern neighbor.

However this may have been, there is no doubt concerning the extended interest taken by the next writer on geographical and historical subjects in matters appertaining to Ethiopia. I refer to Herodotus, who was aptly called by Cicero *"historae patrem,"* or the "Father of History," and who has been rightly termed "the first artist in Greek prose." Like Hecataeus, the "Father of Geography," Herodotus was a Greek, born about 484 B.C. During his life he traveled through

Persia and Palestine and made a long stay in Egypt and in Europe. He talked with all sorts of people, inspected the ruins of fallen civilizations, and noticed the differences between nations. He was quick to note the odd things that distinguished one people from another but was more interested in the deeper and subtler differences that were less apparent.

The results of Herodotus' travels, observations, and enquiries were published in an extensive work called the *Histories*. The second and third books of this great work treat, in the main, of his findings and observations concerning the traditions, history, customs, and civilizations of Egypt and Ethiopia. At Asmara in northern Ethiopia there was discovered an isolated signature of Herodotus, but scholars believe this to be spurious, for Herodotus by his own words does not seem to have traveled during his sojourn in Egypt any farther south than Elephantine, situated near the first cataract which separates Egypt from Ethiopia. He tells us, however, that he made "enquiries concerning the parts beyond," and from the great mass of detailed information which he records concerning Ethiopia (the parts beyond) we may well believe that he not only speaks the truth but that these enquiries were indeed pursued with diligence.

Although Herodotus enjoys, today as he did in antiquity, the distinction of being a kind of titan among ancient historians and one of the most gifted workers who ever applied himself to Clio's craft, he was not always nor is he now universally accorded such an enviable reputation. Strabo, regarding him as hardly more than a compiler of fables, treated his works with marked contempt. There were other writers who showed their disdain by referring to him not as the "Father of History" but as the "Father of Lies." It is true that he had many weaknesses as a historian. He sometimes recorded what were obviously myths and legends without duly indicating that he did not accept them as historic facts; he was often insensible or inattentive to political cause and effect; and he at times accounted for some great event as resulting from some accident without seeking any deeper cause. Of these shortcomings every disinterested and competent student of Herodotus is clearly aware.

It was not these failings, however, which were and are chiefly responsible for the attacks that have been leveled at him by most of his detractors. It was rather the charge that, in his eagerness to tell an interesting and appealing story, he often pieced out his information with undue proportions of inspiration and imagination. And it is perhaps safe to say that in no part of his work was there a greater tendency to credit him with such lapses than in those sections in which he treated Ethiopia and the Ethiopians. In this connection it may be observed that modern scientific and historical research have shown that this attitude towards Herodotus' remarks about the hoary land and its inhabitants is quite ill-founded. In support of this contention I shall, therefore, devote much more time and space to a discussion of certain of these notices than would otherwise be appropriate, paying attention especially to the following points: how modern observations and research have tended to verify their general truth; how some of these notices in particular have greatly extended our own knowledge of Ethiopian history; and how all of them indicate the extent to which facts about Ethiopia had come to be known to the ancient world.

With respect to the natural features of Ethiopia, Herodotus learned from his informants that "as one advances beyond Elephantine [into Ethiopia] the land rises," thus causing the current in the Nile to become "very forceful and swift." He wrote that as one advanced southward the river followed a winding course, and that in one part it divided into two branches, giving rise to an island, and that in other parts the river widened into a magnificent lake on whose shores dwelt Ethiopian nomads.

A fifty-six-day journey south of Syene, a town on the southern frontier of Egypt, led to "a great city called Meroe which is said to be the capital of the other Ethiopians." In the capital of the Ethiopians there was, so Herodotus said, a famous structure called the "table of the Sun". This table reportedly stood "in a meadow in the suburb of the city and was full of boiled flesh of all kinds of animals." The flesh was placed on the great table at night "by those of the citizens who hold office," and "during the day any one who likes can come and eat it." The story of this unique "table of the Sun" for many centuries was regarded as having little or no foundation in fact; Causanias, writing about 147 A.D. treated it as entirely a fable; and that noted student of ancient African civilizations, A. H. Heeren, supposed that merchants may have brought meat and other products to some open market place and that the people left gold in exchange for what they took. The general truth of Herodotus' story seems now, however, to have been confirmed. In 1910 an archeological expedition sponsored by the University of Liverpool excavated near the site of the city of Meroe the ruins of a building which scholars now believe is the self-same "table of the Sun" mentioned by Herodotus. This building, named by its discoverers the "Temple of the Sun", consisted originally of a series of terraces and "on the topmost terrace under the open sky," records the Liverpool Report, "was an altar on which the meats were placed." The archeologists found this temple on the bank of a dry river bed, situated near the edge of the ancient capital, or as Herodotus says, "in a meadow in the suburbs of the city."

Herodotus further stated that in the capital of the Ethiopians there was an oracle dedicated to one of their gods which directed "the warlike expedition of the Ethiopians; when it commands they go to war and in whatever direction it bids them march, thither straightway they carry their arms." In this connection, there is in Ethiopia a number of stelai containing inscriptions which confirm that the Ethiopian form of government was essentially a theocracy, controlled by the priesthood. Indeed some of these inscriptions specifically refer to military expeditions which were undertaken at the special behest of the gods. Hence, there can be no question that Herodotus' statement was in close conformity with the actual truth.

The informants from whom Herodotus derived his information concerning Ethiopia must have been very familiar with conditions and affairs in that kingdom. We stress this fact because there are many other passages in Herodotus' works which have not been as completely verified as those already cited.

Herodotus also related an account of the desertion of "two hundred and forty thousand Egyptian soldiers who went over to the Ethiopians in the reign of King Psammetichus." The cause of this wholesale desertion, says Herodotus, was as follows: Three garrisons were maintained in Egypt at that time; one at Elephantine (on the Ethiopian border) against the Ethiopians; one at Pelusiac Daphnae against the Syrians and Arabians; and a third against the Libyans, in Marea. On one occasion the garrisons were not relieved during a space of three years; thus the soldiers consulted together, determined by common consent to revolt, and marched away towards Ethiopia. Informed of the movement, Psammetichus set out in pursuit and pleaded with them not to desert the gods of their country nor to abandon their wives and children. After arriving in Ethiopia, the deserters placed themselves at the disposal of the king, who made them a present of a tract of land which belonged to certain Ethiopians with whom he was feuding. He bade the deserters to expel the inhabitants and take possession of the territory for themselves. Similar accounts of this episode are also found in the works of Diodorus and Strabo. The names given to the deserters by these writers, however, are different from those used by Herodotus, and in Diodorus a different reason is given for their revolt. It is therefore likely that the later writers drew their accounts from sources other than Herodotus. These considerations would therefore seem to indicate that the story was widespread and must have had some foundation in fact. Moreover, at Abu Sembel in Ethiopia, there is a Greek inscription which was probably written by Greeks who accompanied the Egyptian king in pursuit of the deserters.

As a final instance of the stories related by Herodotus concerning the Ethiopians, I shall now cite what is in many respects perhaps the most valuable of them all, since it incidentally throws much light, if true, on the character of Ethiopian civilization and the physical and cultural characteristics of the peoples of the country in ancient times. This is Herodotus' account of the embassy dispatched to Ethiopia by Cambyses, King of the Persians, during his sojourn in Egypt. An abridged version of Herodotus' account follows.

Cambyses took counsel with himself, and subsequently planned an expedition against the long-lived Ethiopians who dwelt in that part of Libya (applied by Herodotus to the whole of Africa) which borders upon the southern sea. Before attempting to invade Ethiopia, Cambyses planned to send spies into the country under the pretense of carrying presents to the king, but in reality the spies were to take note of all they saw and especially to observe whether there was really what is called the "table of the Sun" in Ethiopia. When Cambyses had made up his mind that the spies should go, he forthwith sent to Elephantine for certain of the Icthyophagi who were acquainted with the Ethiopian language. As soon as the Icthyophagi arrived from Elephantine, Cambyses, having told them what they were to say, forthwith dispatched them into Ethiopia with these gifts: a purple robe, a gold chain for the neck, armlets, an alabaster box of myrrh, and a cask of palm wine. The Ethiopians to whom this embassy was sent were said to be the tallest and handsomest men in the whole world. In their customs they differed greatly from the rest of mankind, and particularly in the way they chose their kings; for they found out the man who was the tallest of all the citizens and of strength equal to his height and appointed him to rule over them.

The Icthyophagi, on reaching this people, delivered the gifts to the king of the country, and spoke as follows: "Cambyses, King of the Persians, anxious to become thy ally and sworn friend, has sent us to hold converse with thee, and to bear these the gifts thou seest, which are the things wherein he himself delights the most." The Ethiopians, who knew they came as spies, answered: "The king of the Persians sent you not with these gifts because he much desired to become my sworn friend, nor is the account which ye give of yourselves true, for ye are come to search out my kingdom. Also your king is not a just man, for were he so, he had not coveted a land which is not his own, nor brought slavery on a people who never did him any wrong. Bear him this bow, and say: 'The king of the Ethiops thus advises the king of the Persians, when the Persians can pull a bow of this strength thus easily [Strabo says the bows of the Ethiopians were four cubits, or six feet, long], then let him come with an army of superior strength against the long-lived Ethiopians; till then, let him thank the gods that they have not put it into the heart of the sons of the Ethiops to covet countries which do not belong to them'."

The spies then were led on a tour and allowed to behold the coffins of the Ethiopians, which were made of crystal, after the following fashion: When the dead body had been dried, either in the Egyptian or in some other manner, they covered the whole with gypsum and adorned it with painting until it was like the living man. Then they placed the body in a crystal pillar which had been hollowed out to receive it, the crystal being dug up in great abundance in their country and very easy to work. One could see the corpse through the pillar; and it did not give any unpleasant odor. The next of kin kept the crystal pillar in their house for a full year from the time of the death, gave it the first fruits continually, and honored it with sacrifices. After the year ended they set the pillar up near the town.

The spies then returned to Egypt and made a report to Cambyses, who was stirred to anger by their words. Forthwith he set out on his march against the Ethiopians, without having made any provisions for the sustenance of the army or reflecting that he was about to wage a major war. At Thebes he detached from his main body some fifty thousand men and sent them against the Ammonians with orders to carry the people into captivity and burn the oracle of Jupiter. Meanwhile, he himself continued with the rest of his forces against the Ethiopians. Before long provisions failed, whereupon the men began to eat the beasts, which shortly failed also. When Cambyses heard of these doings, he gave up his attack on Ethiopia and, retreating by the way he had come, reached Thebes, after he had lost vast numbers of his soldiers. And so ended the expedition against Ethiopia.

For many years much ink flowed from the pens of historians in the attempt to justify or discredit the truth of this story. G. Rawlinson said, "I cannot but think with Niebuhr that both the embassy itself and the account of the Macrobians [the name given by Herodotus to these Ethiopians] are fabulous." Other equally noted writers have been inclined to accept the story as essentially true, though there has been much difference of opinion concerning the part of Ethiopia in which they lived. The German scholar Larcher placed them east of Meroe on the coast of the Red Sea; the traveler James Bruce imagined that he recognized in the tall Shangallas of Ethiopia the modern descendants of these long-lived and great-statured people. Heeren, the celebrated German historian, thought that they were much farther south; he therefore located them beyond the Straits of Bab-el-Mandeb in the neighborhood of Cape Guardafui, and suggested their identification with the modern Somalis.

In the light of more recent research, however, it seems quite probable that the people to whom this story refers are to be identified with the ancient inhabitants who lived in and around the famous city of Meroe. This suggestion is based upon the fact that the story specifically relates that "after they [the members of the embassy] had seen the prison, they were likewise shown what is called the 'table of the Sun'," and as we have seen, there are now very good reasons for believing that this building was the same structure identified with certain ruins discovered near the site of ancient Meroe.

Moreover, gold was beyond any question a most plentiful commodity in the area at that time. In the Asian kingdoms contemporary with the Eighteenth Dynasty there was a belief that gold was in Egypt "as common as dust," and Diodorus recorded a tradition that gold was so plentiful in the country that it was found "lying round in ash piles and dump-heaps." Indeed, all the world from that day to this has held a similar view, yet the truth of the matter is that practically no such precious metal was native to ancient Egypt. The great quantity of gold which circulated in the Land of the Pharaohs was for the most part of Ethiopian origin, and there are many Egyptian documents which shed considerable light on the ways and means by which this precious metal reached the northern kingdom out of the south. In the tomb of Huy, a viceroy in Ethiopia in the reign of King Tutankhamen (c. 1350 B.C.), there is a painting showing the products sent to Egypt by this official. Along with hundreds of other precious things, there is an enormous quantity of gold represented in a variety of forms; in rings, in bags, and sacks of gold dust. A letter dating from the reign of Rameses II (c. 1292–1225 B.C.) addressed to an Egyptian official on duty in Ethiopia instructs this officer to procure for the royal treasury, among other things, "much good gold," including "fans of gold, gold wrought in dishes, and refined gold in bushels." Herodotus said that every third year the Ethiopians sent, among other things, as gifts to the king of the Persians, "two choenices of virgin gold." While these citations have no direct bearing on the truth of Herodotus' statement that Ethiopian prisoners were bound in fetters of gold, yet in the light of the facts given it cannot be denied that the practice was quite within the bounds of possibility.

Concerning Herodotus' statement that the dead were placed in coffins of crystal, archeological research in Ethiopia has as yet revealed no evidence of the existence of such a practice. However, some seeming confirmation does exist. Ctesias of Cindus, a Greek physician living at the court of the Persian King Artaxerxes Memnon in 415–398 B.C., and the author of an anciently famous but long-lost history of Persia and India, has preserved through the pages of Diodorus an interesting notice supplementary to Herodotus' account of burial practices in Ethiopia. The wealthier of the Ethiopians, so the story goes, after embalming the body of the dead, placed it in a hollow statue of gold made to resemble the deceased. The statue was then covered with melted glass and set up in some conspicuous place where it could be viewed for a time by the living relatives. The Ethiopians of lesser fortune followed the same general practice except that the hollowed statue, instead of being made of gold, was composed of silver or of potter's clay.

In another passage Ctesias explains that the far-famed Semeramis, Queen of Assyria, after having subdued many places in Asia and Egypt, turned her attention to Ethiopia.

Here she had an opportunity to see "a four square lake a hundred and sixty feet in circuit, the water of which was extraordinarily sweet and of color like unto vermilion. It sent forth a delicate odor like old wine and was of such wonderful efficacy that whoever drank of it went mad and acknowledged all the sins which he had long since committed and forgotten." It long has been customary for scholars, following the lead of Lucian, to treat Ctesias' writings as hardly more than a collection of wintertales, and among the episodes he relates are some which most assuredly may be fairly classed as such. But in this connection, it may be pointed out that the excavations at Meroe by the Liverpool expedition revealed evidence which suggests that there may be some truth in this part of his story. There have been discovered not only the remains of elaborately constructed baths and beautifully decorated swimming pools, but in one of the pools there has been found a column of plaster within whose center is embedded an earthenware pipe apparently designed to convey water through the column. The pipe is threaded through the column, says W. S. George, the engineer of the expedition, and is similar in character to other pipes which were used in connection with the heating and conveying of the water through the baths; however, it is smaller than the pipes used for such purposes, and such pipes are not embedded in columns of plaster. This pipe-threaded column, therefore, must have had some other use. George hinted that it might once have stood upright in the pool and, by some system of hydraulics, water may have been forced up through the column to its top, thus producing a fountain-like cascade in the center of the pool. With such a pool in mind, and by assuming that the waters used in the baths were treated with some aromatic spices or salts for which Ethiopia has long been noted, it becomes easy enough to believe that Herodotus' account of the violet-scented fountain could very well have had some foundation in truth.

Finally, Herodotus in all likelihood spoke the truth when he indicated that the Ethiopian king admonished the members of Cambyses' embassy to tell their master to "thank the gods that they have not put into the hearts of the sons of the Ethiops to covet countries which do not belong to them." It is true that in almost every instance where we are able to get a glimpse into the character of the Ethiopian sovereigns, great warriors though they were, we find them free of those rapacious and piratic habits that have so often sullied the otherwise brilliant careers of so many monarchs of other nations. The conquest of Egypt by the Ethiopian king Piankhy in the eighth century B.C. was in its origin no greedy imperialistic undertaking but a movement made necessary by the threatening attempt of the Egyptians to seize Ethiopian territory. And in his triumphant march through Egypt, we are told that before he would attack a city he would first offer it the most favorable terms of peace to avoid fighting, for it was his desire that harm should come to no one, that "not even a babe might have cause to cry." If this policy failed, he took the city but guarded it against undue plunder and destruction at the hands of his soldiers; and when he left Egypt to return to Ethiopia "he did not leave behind a land filled with the slain and the ruins of towns which he had burned," nor were there "fields blackened with the ashes of the crops which he had set on fire."

The spirit of tolerance and forebearance was also evident on the part of Piankhy's successor, Shabaka; the same statesmanlike qualities are expressed in the activities of the Ethiopian king Tarhaka during his reign over Egypt. Diodorus ascribed a similar humanitarian character to Actisanes, another Ethiopian king of Egypt who cannot now be otherwise identified; and Heliodorus, in his celebrated novel *Aethiopica*, presented a like picture in his delineation of the, character of Hydapses, the Ethiopian king upon whom much of his famous story centers. Here were true representatives of Homer's "blameless" and Hesiod's "high-souled Ethiopians." Hence, Herodotus' account of the Ethiopian king's rebuke to Cambyses for his evil designs is quite in keeping with what history and tradition record as being a common policy of the sovereigns of that time. It is therefore not impossible to believe that this incident in the story had some foundation in fact.

Such, then, is the character and status of some of the more notable and typical notices which Herodotus has preserved concerning ancient Ethiopia. Time was when the Herodotian sidelights on Ethiopia's past were regarded as hardly more than graceful and gratuitous fictions from first to last, but modern discovery and research are changing such opinions. The student in quest of antiquities of an Ethiopian cast will find the Father of History an invaluable guide to the prosecution of his task.

The century in which Herodotus flourished and the four centuries which followed comprised the Golden Age of ancient geographical and historical literature, and throughout this long period Ethiopia continued to be a favorite topic with many of the most gifted writers who labored in these and related fields. Unfortunately, the majority of the works of this period which are known to have treated of Ethiopia are now lost. Through references, epitomes, excerpts, citations, and the like taken from many of these treatises and preserved in other classical works still extant, it is possible to speak with a fair degree of certainty concerning the character and content of these Ethiopian notices.

## DIODORUS SICULUS

Diodorus Siculus was a Greek born on the island of Sicily about the end of the second or the beginning of the first century B.C. Following a resolution to write a general history of mankind, he spent some thirty years in study and travel to groom himself for his ambitious task. According to his own testimony, he undertook many laborious and dangerous journeys in Europe, Asia, and Africa in order to acquaint himself personally with the lands whose history and civilizations he would endeavor to record and describe. His efforts culminated in a voluminous work to which he gave the comprehensive title *Bibliotheca Historica*, or *The Historical Library*. This work, published sometime between 59 and 30 B.C., originally comprised forty books, but of these only fifteen have been preserved.

As a historian, Diodorus is generally charged with having been unmethodical in his plan and deficient in the critical judgment in the selection and use of his materials. Fortunately for us, however, it is the scholarly consensus that one of the most trustworthy and valuable parts of his work is the section in which he treats of the history and civilization of the Ethiopians. This conclusion is warranted because many of the statements which he makes in this connection have since been verified by the research of modern archeologists and anthropologists.

Diodorus, it appears, never traveled in Ethiopia; it may therefore, at first sight, be a bit surprising that his account of that ancient land should turn out to be one of the most reliable sections of his extended work. However, this fact is easily explained when we take into account the sources upon which he drew for his information. According to his own testimony, he derived 'he major portion of his information concerning Ethiopia from four sources: first, the writings of Agathar-

chides; second, the works of Artemidorus; third, through in-
quiries made of native Egyptians informed on Ethiopian
matters; and fourth, from interviews with many important
Ethiopians whom it was his good fortune to meet during his
sojourn in Egypt. Before taking up the specific character of
Diodorus' Ethiopian notices, a brief biographical sketch will
be given of the two authors to whom Diodorus acknowledges
his special indebtedness.

Agatharchides, a Greek, was a native of Cindus in Asia
Minor but lived during the latter part of his life, the closing
decades of the second century B.C., at Alexandria where he
served as tutor and advisor to the youthful Ptolemy Soter II,
who was then king of Egypt. He is known to have been the
author of extensive works treating of both Asia and Europe,
but of these only a few meager fragments survive. He also
wrote, during his residence in Egypt, a treatise in five books
concerning the Red Sea and the nations adjoining it, but this
too, in its original form, is now lost. A survey of the contents
of two of these books, the fourth and the fifth, have survived
in the form of an abstract made of them by Photius. The abstract reveals that it was from this work of Agatharchides that
Diodorus secured his information about Ethiopia on the Red
Sea. As a resident of Egypt, and through his important position as tutor and advisor to the king, Agatharchides may be
supposed to have enjoyed unrivaled means and opportunities
for acquiring information concerning the African countries of
which he wrote, and from a study of his writings this seems
indeed to have been the case. His notices of the manners and
customs of the Ethiopians of the eastern desert, though containing some statements that might be seriously questioned,
have been to a large extent confirmed as substantially true by
modern observations. Upon the then much debated question
of the cause of the inundations of the Nile, Agatharchides entertained sound views; his explanation was that they were the

result of heavy and continuous rains taking place in the mountains of Ethiopia.

It is said that Agatharchides was "acquainted with the language of the Ethiopians." Considering the opportunities which he had at his command for gathering information and the critical method which he pursued, we can only regret that digests of but two of his books have survived. E. H. Bunbury places these "among the most valuable of the minor geographical writings that remain from antiquity." We do not know the contents of his other three books, but some scholars believe that they dealt with the civilization of the much celebrated Ethiopians who lived on the Island of Meroe. Bunbury thinks that Diodorus may have drawn much of his information concerning inhabitants of that region from those lost works and suggests that the reliability of his account concerning these people may be attributed to that fact.

Of Artemidorus, the second author to whom Diodorus acknowledges his indebtedness, only a brief statement need be made. We are told that he was a native of Ephesus but, like Agatharchides, he is said to have studied and written at Alexandria in Egypt. His principal work was a general treatise on geography, but this work is known to us now mainly from digests made of it by Marcian of Heraclea (third century A.D.) and from citations in the works of Diodorus and Strabo. The section devoted to Africa, upon which Diodorus drew, seems to have been a treatise on the Ethiopians, the eastern desert, and Meroe and its environs. There is also a valuable account of the ports along the African shores of the Red Sea as well as a detailed description of the coast of Africa from the Straits of Bab-el-Mandeb southward as far as Cape Guardafui. The writings of Artemidorus are said to have enjoyed a considerable reputation in ancient times, and modern scholars hold that their systematic character and general accuracy thoroughly justified such consideration. Here, then, is another reason for the trustworthiness of those parts of Diodorus' work treating of Ethiopia.

Before passing on to our summary of the specific notices given by Diodorus concerning the history, customs, and manners of the Ethiopians, I wish again to call attention to his statement that much of his information was derived from Ethiopians with whom he associated while in Egypt. This is a most significant consideration, for we know from other sources, mainly archeological, that Ethiopian civilization was at this period (first century B.C.) in a most flourishing condition. Commercial and social relations between Egypt and her southern neighbor were then extensive, and there was political peace between the two countries. The Greek rulers of Egypt and the Ethiopian sovereigns held each other in high regard and frequently exchanged gifts as tokens of their friendship. Numbers of Greeks traveled, and some made their residence, in Ethiopia, and Ethiopian emissaries are known to have been frequent visitors in the cities and towns of Egypt. Under such circumstances it is easy enough to believe that Diodorus' informants, as well as those interrogated by Agatharchides and Artemidorus, were men of high station in their native country and were therefore competent and capable of supplying reliable information about their native land.

Diodorus is credited with saying that the Ethiopians informed him that they were the oldest people in the world; that they originated religious worship and the practices of making sacrifices to the gods; that the habitable parts of Egypt were formed of mud brought down from their country by the River Nile; that the earliest Egyptians were colonists from Ethiopia; and that the Egyptians borrowed many of their religious beliefs and cultural practices from the Ethiopians. Modern investigation and research have shown that there is a substantial amount of truth in all of these claims.

Diodorus has also preserved a series of ancient traditions:

that in very ancient times there were mighty kingdoms and empires in the inner regions of Africa, which were wont, on occasion, to send forth vast armies which brought many parts of the world under their subjection, and these traditions, modern archeological research also has revealed, were apparently founded upon considerable historical truth.

In yet another place Diodorus' work holds that the stories about Osiris of the Egyptians and Dionysus of the Greeks were but glorified editions of occurrences and exploits originally experienced and perfomed by a real prince belonging to an old royal family of inner Africa. In this connection the descriptions of the region in which this prince is said by tradition to have spent his earlier years was situated within the realm of Ethiopia.

We now turn to a brief review of matters relating to Diodorus' observations concerning the geography of Ethiopia. Of the Nile, Diodorus wrote that "it runs from the south towards the north from spring heads—that are in the utmost borders of Ethiopia. Flowing down from the mountains of Ethiopia, making way through many countries, some fertile and some vast deserts fierce with heat, and after many large turnings and windings it passes into Egypt and finally empties itself into the sea." The river "runs calm and smooth without any violent surges or tempestuous waves except at the cataracts." At these cataracts (the largest of which, as Diodorus rightly says, was on the borders of Ethiopia and Egypt, the great Second Cataract), there are in the river's bed "many great stones like huge rocks."

In the course of its windings and turnings through Ethiopia, the river, wrote Diodorus, "often divides in such a way as to make many islands; the largest and most remarkable of which is called Meroe," or the Island of Meroe. This "island is three thousand furlongs in length and a thousand in breadth and was said to have the shape of a shield." To the west of the island on the Libyan side are "vast heaps of sand which come down close to the river" that runs eastward towards Arabia "run along steep rocky mountains. . . in the island is a famous city called Meroe—and in other parts are mines of gold, silver, iron, and brass; a great quantity of ebony trees and all sorts of precious stones." It is hardly necessary to say that modern observations and research have sustained the general truth of the foregoing statements in almost every detail.

In reporting his interviews with the Ethiopian ambassadors whom he met in Egypt, Diodorus relates that these dignitaries informed him that the Ethiopians had "always been a free people and had never been brought into subjection by any foreign prince," and this notwithstanding the fact that many powerful rulers of other lands had sought to invade their country. In this connection, the Ethiopians mentioned particularly the failure of efforts of this kind which had been made by Assyria and also by Cambyses, the king of Persia. It was also stated that Hercules and Dionysus who in more ancient days "ran through the whole world" had nevertheless made no attempt to subjugate Ethiopia, for they were not only awed by the piety of its people but realized the great difficulties which would be confronted in any effort to conquer that nation.

In the Twelfth Dynasty, as the Egyptian records attest, northern Ethiopia, or the region between the first and third cataracts, came under the rule of Egypt, and an echo of this is also preserved by Diodorus. The notice is an account of how a great Egyptian king named Sesostris (Sesostris I) "marched against the Ethiopians inhabiting the south and having conquered them, forced them to pay him tribute of ebony, gold and elephants' teeth."

Many years afterwards, there came to the throne of Egypt, according to Diodorus, a king named Annoses "who carried himself tyranically towards his subjects. . . . He put many to death against all law and justice and as many he stripped of all they had, turned them out of their estates, and carried himself haughtily and proudly towards all people with whom he had to deal. This the people endured for a time, but when Actisanes, king of Ethiopia, attacked him, most of his subjects revolted, so that he was easily conquered and Egypt became subject to the kings of Ethiopia. After this king's death the Egyptians recovered their liberty (from the Ethiopians) and set up a king of their own nation to rule over them."

Equally as interesting is yet another story, which Diodorus has preserved, concerning another king of the south. This is the story of a king styled by Diodorus "Sabach," but who is known as Shabaka and who reigned over Ethiopia and Egypt about the end of the eighth century B.C. Of this king Diodorus said that he went "beyond all his predecessors in his worship of the gods, and kindness to his subjects." He allegedly abolished the death penalty and "made an edict whereby the condemned persons were placed in chains and put to work raising levees and digging many commodious canals, for by this means, as the king perceived, he not only moderated the sentence of the condemned but advanced the public good as well."

Of the Ethiopians who dwelt in Meroe and in those tracts that lie next to Egypt, Diodorus wrote that "a great part of their laws differ in many ways from those of other nations, especially those which concern the election of their kings." When a new king was to be selected and elevated, it was, said our author, "their custom to bring together the best of their priests out of every rank and order and as these passed before the god the Divinity would select by a laying on of hands one from among this number for the regal office." When the king had been thus designated, the people would "forthwith fall down upon their knees and worship him as a god and render him other honors as he to whom the authority of the chief

magistrate is committed by divine providence.... Being so
elected, he never conferred rewards, nor inflicted punishment
upon any except in accordance with the ancient laws ratified
and approved by his ancestors from the beginning."

Regarding the specific character of some of these laws,
Diodorus wrote that it was a custom, or law, among the Ethiopians that no subject who had been condemned to die was
actually executed by the officials of the state "though he be
ever so guilty." Nor was it lawful to escape punishment "by
willful banishment or by fleeing into other countries as was
the custom among the Greeks." In this connection the author
related that he was told by the Ethiopians that on one occasion there was a subject who, after he had been presented
with the sign of death, was detected "preparing to flee out of
Ethiopia. His own mother, however, discerning his design,
fastened her garter about his neck and he underwent all till
he was strangled to death."

One of the most interesting and historically significant
passages in Diodorus is the following statement concerning
the power given to priests by Ethiopian law and custom over
even the king of the country. "The priests," says the passage,
"who are employed in the service of the gods at Meroe exercised the greatest authority. For they could whensoever they
pleased, send a messenger to the king commanding him in the
name of the god to put himself to death." The force of the
custom was so strong that "for many ages no king ever dared
to resist the priestly orders, but observed their dictates without force or compulsion." Evidently, however, there did come
to the throne a king who was bold enough to resist and break
the ancient custom. This was Ergamenes who "reigned in the
time of Ptolemy the Second" (of Egypt, end of third century
B.C.). When the fatal priestly order came to Ergamenes, "this
prince, assuming the spirit and courage becoming a king,
marched with a considerable body of men to the place where

stood the golden temple of the Ethiopians and there cut the throats of all the priests." Having abolished this ancient custom through such severe and revolutionary means, Ergamenes then "reformed what appertained to the service of the gods in such a manner as he saw fit."

Continuing his theme on the manners and polity of the Ethiopians, Diodorus further related that he was informed that there was still another ancient law among them that was even "more strange and wonderful." This law or custom provided that if the sovereign should become "maimed or debilitated upon any occasion in any member of his body, . . . the great officers of the king as well as his household servants, do the same thing to themselves. For they hold it a base and unworthy thing, that if the king be lame, that they should attend upon him with whole and sound limbs. It is moreover a custom for the king's domestic servants to put themselves to death when their royal master dies, and such death they account honorable and as a testimony of their sincere love for their prince."

Clearly, Diodorus must be regarded as a significant source, when studying the culture of the ancient Ethiopians.

## STRABO THE GEOGRAPHER

Next on the list of classical authors with whom we are concerned is Strabo, the geographer, one of the most remarkable scholars of antiquity. From the meager knowledge that has survived concerning his personal history it appears that Strabo was born about the year 63 B.C. in Amasia, the capital of the celebrated kingdom of Pontus on the Black Sea. He is thought to have died about the end of the first quarter of the first century A.D. At the time of his

birth his native city was characterized by a strong tincture of
Greek civilization and was doubtless the seat of a large Greek
population. From the fact that certain members of his family
are known to have held important military and political posts,
it appears certain that Strabo's youth was spent in favorable
and cultured surroundings. Early in his life he became a pupil
of Aristodemus, the tutor of the sons of Pompey the Great,
and afterwards he studied at Rome under Tyrannion, noted as
an authority on geography and as the teacher of Cicero's two
sons, Marcus and Quintus. Subsequently he studied philosophy under the Aristotlian Xenarchus who "enjoyed the
friendship of Areius and later of Augustus Caesar."

Although Strabo's fame today rests upon his endeavors
as a geographer, his first efforts in the field of productive
scholarship were as a historian, and it is as such that he seems
to have been best known in his own age. The work which
won for him this distinction, an extensive historical treatise
in forty-three books to which he gave the title *Historical
Memoirs*, has long since been lost, but it is mentioned by
Plutarch and was extensively used by both Josephus and
Arrian. Strabo himself refers to it by name in his geographical writings, and it is thought by some that many of the historical notices which he so frequently includes in these are
doubtless summaries taken from this earlier work. If Strabo's
attainments as a historian were of the standard he achieved
as a geographer, scholars may well lament that the work of
his first love is no longer preserved, for his *Geography*, as
it is more commonly known, was regarded by no less competent a critic than Bunbury as "not only the most important geographical work that has come down to us from
antiquity but it is unquestionably one of the most important
ever produced by any Greek or Roman writer."

This remarkable treatise, however, unlike his historical
work, does not seem to have been known to his great succes-

sors in this field. Neither it nor its author is mentioned by
Pliny, who flourished only a half-century later, nor is any allusion to it found in the great work of Claudius Ptolemy. It
has been supposed that this is to be explained on the grounds
that the *Geography* was perhaps completed and published in
Strabo's native Amasia which, notwithstanding its historical
connections, was remote from the great centers of learning of
that day. But however this may be, by the Middle Ages the
work had become widely and favorably known; and by the
scholars of that time its author was spoken of as *the* geographer. And although the searching analysis of the higher
geographical criticism of our times has revealed the *Geography*
to contain some glaring defects, there are still sufficient
grounds for taking the stand with Bunbury that this is the
most important treatise of its kind ever penned by a classical
author.

Alexander von Humboldt has written that Strabo's work
surpassed all other geographical labors of antiquity by the
grandeur of its composition and by the diversity of its subjects, and this is hardly an overstatement, for in no other
volume that has come down from ancient times is one likely
to find so varied an assortment of geographical and historical
matters so systematically and artistically presented as in the
seventeen books which comprise this great composition. The
first sixteen of these books are devoted to a survey of the geography and history of Europe and Asia, and the seventeenth
surveys parts of Africa. In this last, the greater part of the discussion centers on Egypt and Ethiopia, and in the first and
sixteenth books there are also several lengthy passages devoted to the Ethiopians. Scattered through several of the other
books are also numerous brief references and notices of these
ancient people. Moreover, those sections of the seventeenth
book treating Egypt and Ethiopia are said by Bunbury to be
"on the whole the most complete and satisfactory portions" of

Strabo's entire work. Needless to say, such an observation concerning so celebrated a work is most enheartening to the student of Ethiopian history.

If we examine the character of the sources and the circumstances under which Strabo acquired his information concerning Ethiopia, it is not surprising that what he has to say of that ancient country was, on the whole, quite trustworthy. As in the case of Herodotus and Diodorus, Strabo does not seem to have personally visited Ethiopia, but like his two predecessors he did spend quite some time in Egypt. Much of his sojourn there was passed at Alexandria, but in the years 25–24 B.C. he accompanied his friend and patron, Aelius Gallus, then the Roman governor of Egypt, on an extended tour of the country which carried him as far south as the borders of Ethiopia. Only a few years before Strabo's visit to the Ethiopian border, matters had been such as to center the attention of the Romans on Ethiopia. After the battle of Actium in 31–30 B.C., causing the fall of the Ptolemaic dynasty and the conversion of Egypt into a Roman province, one of the last acts of Cleopatra before the fateful event, was to send her son Caesarion, son of Julius Caesar, and her two children by Antony, down to the south "in the hope that in Ethiopia they would find shelter and support against Rome."

In 29 B.C. the Roman governor of Egypt, Cornelius Gallus, and the Ethiopians met for the purpose of settling the question of the boundary between Roman Egypt and Ethiopia; and in 23–22 B.C., the year following Strabo's visit to the border and while he was doubtless still in Egypt, the Ethiopians invaded Upper Egypt and routed a number of Roman garrisons stationed there. Following hard on this, Gaius Petronius, the newly appointed prefect of Egypt, retaliated by marching with an army into Ethiopia where he captured and sacked a number of Ethiopian towns and cities, among them the great city of Napata, which for more than a thousand years had

been one of the leading metropolises of the southern kingdom. Under circumstances such as these, it is conceivable that
Strabo was able to acquire a goodly amount of what was practically firsthand information concerning the land and its
people.

In addition to this, Strabo, by his own testimony, drew
heavily on the works of previous authors who had written of
the country. He specifically mentions his indebtedness to Artemidorus and Eratosthenes. The first of these, from whom he
drew the bulk of his information concerning the people of the
eastern desert, we have already discussed in the section on
Diodorus; of the second, Eratosthenes, we may well pause for
a moment or two to include a brief introductory remark.

Eratosthenes was born in the North African city of Cyrene about the year 276 B.C. Around 240 B.C. he was appointed
to the headship of the great library at Alexandria, a post
which he held with distinction for more than forty years. In
the course of his life, he wrote a number of books, of both a
literary and scientific character, that placed his name high in
the ancient world of letters, but unfortunately all of these
have perished. Among his writings was a treatise on geography which, to judge from the surviving fragments and
notices of it contained in the later works of authors, was one
of the most systematic and reliable efforts of the kind ever at-
tempted in ancient times. In this work there was apparently a
rather extensive section treating Ethiopia, and according to
Bunbury, the greater part of the information recorded by Eratosthenes in this connection was derived from the Ethiopians
themselves. And when it is remembered that Ethiopia was ex-
periencing at this very time what has been called the golden
age of its civilization, it is not surprising that Eratosthenes
was able, by interrogating Ethiopians, to render an account of
certain features of the country which we now know to be
remarkably close to the truth.

It is of interest to note that Strabo mentions two works specifically devoted to the Nile written by two of his contemporaries, one named Endorus and the other Aristo. Both of these authors, except for Strabo's references, are otherwise totally unknown. Though he said he read and compared each of their works, he has not explained whether he was indebted to them for any information concerning Ethiopia.

Strabo nowhere mentions that he was familiar with the Ethiopian references contained in the writings of Herodotus or Diodorus, but when it is remembered that he considered Herodotus as essentially a collector of fables, this is not surprising. There are in his work, however, allusions to some of the same Ethiopian events and episodes recorded by these earlier writers. That Strabo drew upon them without having the courtesy to give them credit is hardly likely; the similarities are more probably to be explained on the grounds that the incidents and events on which they center were a part of the stock knowledge and traditions of the times and were hence derived from sources independent of either of the two previously mentioned authors.

Having before us these observations on the sources from which Strabo drew much of his information, we may now turn to a brief review of some of the specific references to the land and peoples of Ethiopia. Concerning the course of the Nile and its tributaries, Strabo, guided by the map of Eratosthenes and doubtless by fresh information supplied by the Ethiopian expedition of Petronius, clearly describes not only the great S-shaped curve made by the river between Meroe and the second cataract but also gives a rather accurate account of the formation of the Island of Meroe by the junction of the Atbara and the Blue Nile. Though he was not entirely clear on its exact relation, Strabo also mentioned another Ethiopian river, the Astapus, "as a part of the Nile system"; this river, so he was informed, "issues out of some lakes in the south." Here Strabo is evidently referring to the White Nile. Strabo also wrote that beyond Meroe was "Pesbo, a large lake containing a well inhabited island," the reference here being, as is generally agreed, to Lake Tana, in the heart of Ethiopia, which is the source of the Blue Nile. Strabo was the first of the ancient geographers to mention this lake, a feature in the geography of this part of Africa, which was not to be verified by modern Europeans until the eighteenth century. Regarding the inundation of the Nile, which he graphically described, Strabo stated that in his day it was well known that this phenomenon was caused by "the summer rains which fall in great abundance in upper Ethiopia, particularly in the most distant mountains. When the rains ceased," he further observed, "the fullness of the river gradually subsides."

On the location of the great city of Meroe, Strabo was likewise correctly informed; it was, he said, on the Island of Meroe and was situated, "above [south of] the confluence of the Astaboras [Atbara] and the Nile at the distance of 700 stadia" [about seventy miles]. This city was the "largest royal seat" of the Ethiopians, and modern archeological observations and excavations have verified this statement, for Meroe at that time was larger than Napata, the second of the royal Ethiopian cit- ies. "The houses in the cities," Strabo further noted, "are formed by interweaving split pieces of palm wood or of bricks." The observation concerning the use of bricks for the building of houses has likewise been demonstrated as a fact by archeological operations.

Regarding the customs of the Ethiopians, Strabo explained that they selected their kings from among persons distinguished for their personal beauty, riches, or courage; and that the Ethiopians "reverence their kings as gods, who are for the most part shut up in their palaces." The truth of the statement that the kingship was not strictly hereditary and that people had a hand in the selection is vouchsafed by certain Ethiopian inscriptions, and the reverence paid to the kings and the practice of royalty shielding itself from public view are in keeping with customs which are known to have been widespread in Africa from most ancient times down to our own day.

Strabo also has a version of Diodorus' observation on the former power of the priests: "In Meroe the priests anciently held the highest rank and sometimes sent orders even to the king by a messenger, to put an end to himself when they appointed another king in his place. At last one of their kings abolished this custom by going with an armed body to the temple where the golden shrine is, and slaughtering all the priests." Here we have an echo of the theocratic form of government which is described in more detail in previously quoted passages from Herodotus and Diodorus and in the accounts concerning the election of the king that are preserved on the coronation stele of Aspalta and in the annals of Nastasen.

In addition to such observations on the character and influence of the religion of the Ethiopians, Strabo relates more specifically that "They [the Ethiopians] regard as God one being who is immortal and the cause of all things. There is another who is mortal, a being without a name, whose nature is not clearly understood." Strabo further wrote that the Ethiopians, in general, consider also as gods "benefactors and royal persons, some of whom are their kings, the common saviors and guardians of all; others are private persons, esteemed as gods by those who have individually received benefits from them. Of those who inhabit torrid regions, some are even supposed not to acknowledge any god and are said to abhor even the sun and apply opprobrious names to him [the sun god] when they behold him rising because he scorches and tortures them with his heat."

Concerning the burial of the dead, some of the Ethiopians, according to Strabo, "enclose them in *hyalus;* some bury them around the temples in coffins of baked clay. They swear an oath by them which is reverenced as more sacred than all others." The material *hyalus* has not been definitely identified (perhaps it was the glass-like material mentioned by Herodotus and Diodorus); but the statement that some of the dead were buried "around the temples" has been verified by John Garstang's discovery of a great cemetery in the neighborhood of the temple area at Meroe.

In addition to the inhabitants of Meroe, Strabo mentioned several other groups, the most noted of which were "the fugitive Egyptians who revolted in the time of Psammetichus and who are called the Sembritae or foreigners." They occupied, he said, "another island above Meroe," probably Sennar, the territory between the Blue and White Niles; "their sovereign is a queen but they obey the king of Meroe." A second group (and here Strabo quotes from Eratosthenes) is "the Nubae," the modern Nubians, who lived on the left bank of the Nile opposite Meroe. Strabo also referred to two other groups, the latter of which was destined to figure prominently in the subsequent history of Ethiopia and Roman Egypt. These were "the Megabari and the Blemmyes, who are subject to the Ethiopians and border upon the Egyptians."

Concerning the natural products of Ethiopia, Strabo observed that "there are mines of copper, iron, gold and various kinds of precious stone." There were also deposits of "fossil salt as in Arabia." Of the flora he wrote, "Palm, the persea, ebony and carob trees are found in great abundance." The persea, a species of the genus to which the common peach tree belongs, explained Strabo, "is a lofty tree and its fruit is large and sweet." Diodorus said it was introduced into Egypt from Ethiopia. The somewhat unfamiliar carob tree has evergreen pennate leaves and small red petalless flowers; it bears a long

pod which contains a sweetish pulp which is used for stock
and is sometimes eaten by man.

Strabo's list of Ethiopian animals included in the domestic
series, the ox, the cow, the goat, the sheep, and the dog. Concerning the sheep, he noted that instead of wool they "have
hair like goats"; and of the dogs, "they are small, though
fierce and quarrelsome." Among the wild animals were the
elephant, the baboon, the lion, the panther, the ostrich, the
rhinoceros, the camel, and the leopard. Of the last four, Strabo
gave some quite interesting accounts and descriptions which I
cannot resist passing on here. The first relates the method
pursued by the people of the eastern desert in capturing the
ostrich. "Some hunt them with bows and arrows, covered
with the skins of birds. They hide the right hand in the neck
of the skin and move it as the birds move their necks. With
the left hand they scatter grain from a bag suspended to the
side; thus they entice the birds, until they drive them into pits
where the hunters despatch them with cudgels. The skins are
used both as clothes and as covering for beds."

There is still another passage in which Strabo gives from
his own personal observation a notice of an Ethiopian animal.
This is his peculiarly charming account of the sacred hawk
which he saw in the temple at Philae during his visit to the
Ethiopian border. The passage, incidentally, also throws a
valuable bit of light on what was a widespread Ethiopian and
Egyptian religious practice. In one of the temples at Philae,
the account holds, "a bird which they [the Egyptians and Ethi-
opians] call the hierax [the hawk] is worshipped. But it did not
appear to me to resemble in the least the hawks of our
country nor of Egypt, for it was larger and very different in
the marks of its plumage. They said that the bird was Ethiopian and is brought from Ethiopia when its predecessor dies,
or before its death. The one shown to us when we were there
was sick and nearly dead."

The hawk was sacred, one of the oldest, most important, and most widely worshipped gods in the Nile Valley. Temples erected to this deity and statues and reliefs of it are found throughout Egypt and Ethiopia. In most instances, the god is represented with the body of a man but the head of a hawk. According to one Egyptian tradition preserved in the myth of Horus, this deity seems to have been of Ethiopian origin. In the light of these facts the foregoing passage of Strabo is particularly significant.

With regard to the more strictly historical notices given by Strabo concerning Ethiopia, the following two are worthy of special mention. The first is his statement that "when Cambyses was in possession of Egypt he advanced with the Egyptians as far as Meroe and it is said that he gave this name both to the island [Island of Meroe] and to the city, because his sister [according to some writers, his wife] Meroe died there." By implying that the Persian army reached Meroe, and in ascribing the origin of the name Meroe to Cambyses, he adds features not found in the version given by Herodotus. Since Herodotus' account was written less than a hundred years after the event while Strabo's was composed almost exactly five hundred years after, the probabilities are that the earlier version is nearer the truth, and Strabo's additions may be put down as accretions which the story had gathered with age.

But if Strabo is to be distrusted here, there is nevertheless another statement of his that may be safely regarded as perhaps the most reliable and most valuable historical notice concerning Ethiopia in any of the works of the classical authors. This is his long and interesting account of the Ethiopian attack on the Roman forts in Egypt and the invasion staged in retaliation by the Romans under Petronius. These events occurred the year following Strabo's visit to the Ethiopian border, and it is quite possible that Strabo was still in Egypt at the time. This being the case, it is not impossible that Strabo gathered his details from eyewitnesses of, and perhaps even actual participants in, the affrays.

Under such circumstances it need not be surprising that this is the longest and most detailed single historical notice concerning either Egypt or Ethiopia given by the celebrated geographer. In one place the text says that when the Ethiopians attacked the Roman garrisons, they "threw down the statues of Caesar," and in another place it is implied that these were carried away to Ethiopia. In this connection, it is most interesting to note that in 1914 the Liverpool Expedition, excavating at Meroe, unearthed a bronze head which appeared to be a portrait of Caesar, and members of the expedition have suggested that it may be one of those to which Strabo referred. Another passage states that when the Romans invaded Ethiopia, "Petronius attacked and took Napata . . . and razed it." Most interesting in this connection is the fact that when G. A. Reisner of the Harvard-Boston Expedition was excavating the ruins of the great Ethiopian temples near Napata, he found what is thought to be evidence of the damages wrought by the Romans. In the walls of the great Temple of Piankhy there are traces of what appear to be repairs of just such destruction as the Romans might have caused. Moreover, there was also discovered on one of the walls an inscription, placed there by the Ethiopian sovereign who reigned only a decade or so after Strabo's time, which specifically states that he made extensive restorations in the great temple. It may also be noted that the Liverpool Expedition discovered at Meroe in 1914 a long inscription written in the as yet ill-understood Meroitic script, which has been tentatively interpreted as an Ethiopian version of the conflict with the Romans. Thus modern archeology seems bent on providing a solid confirmation of Strabo's most celebrated historical notice.

PLINY THE ELDER

P liny the Elder, or Pliny the Naturalist, is the next
man on the roll of classical authors to be considered.
The other writers who have been discussed were
Greeks, but Pliny was a Roman, and his is by far the most important Latin work to which we shall have occasion to refer in
this survey. Through the fortunate survival of notices concerning him, the personal history of Pliny the Elder is fairly
well known, although some outstanding details of his life are
obscure. It is generally agreed that he was born of a wealthy
and noble parentage in the year 23 A.D.; the place of his birth,
however, is a matter of dispute. Some scholars assign him to
the town of Novum Conum (the modern Como) in the north
of Italy, while others think that Verona was his birthplace. It
is well established that he died at the age of fifty-six in 79 A.D.

At the age of twenty-three Pliny became a soldier in the
wars against the Teutonic "barbarians," and for the rest of his
life was almost continuously employed on active duty in the
service of the state. In the reign of Uro he served as procura-
tor in Spain and he held a high place at the imperial court. He
seems also to have been connected with the imperial treasury,
and at the time of his death in the reign of Titus, with whom
he was likewise on the most intimate terms, he was in command of an important division of the Roman fleet.

Notwithstanding the demands which such positions of re-
sponsibility must have made upon his time and energy, Pliny
was able to devote himself to an active literary career that was
destined to place his name very high in the world of ancient
letters. By his contemporaries he was regarded as one of the
most learned men of his age, and posterity has come to regard
him as one of the most diligent students and most voluminous
writers of, ancient times. His industry and resourcefulness is
clearly reflected in the long list of works that are to be placed

to his credit: these include a biography of *Pomponius Secundus* in two books; a history of the wars in Germany in twenty books; a monumental work on education entitled, *The Student*, in six volumes; a similar work *On Difficulties in the Latin Language* in eight books; a history of Rome in thirty-one books; and finally, his most renowned composition, *Natural History (Historic Naturalis)* in thirty-seven books. Of this long list, only the *Natural History* has survived, but this alone is sufficient to insure the perpetuation of Pliny's name and fame as a student and writer for all time. This celebrated work, published about 77 A.D. and dedicated to the Emperor Titus, is easily classed as one of the most valuable treatises that has come down to us from antiquity. In the words of his celebrated nephew—an opinion which most modern scholars have accepted—"it is a work remarkable for its comprehensiveness and erudition and no less varied than Nature herself."

The *Natural History* is not a natural history in the modern connotation of the term but rather a vast encyclopedia of ancient knowledge and belief on almost every known subject of that day. Some twenty thousand different topics of importance are discussed, among them questions of so varied a character as the origin and nature of the universe, the character of the civilizations and the leading geographical features of various countries of the inhabited world, the peculiarities of different peoples of the earth, the habits and characteristics of birds, fish, and wild beasts, the diseases of domesticated animals and their remedies, the number of eggs to be put under brood hens; he discusses the liver of a fat goose and the fondness of bats for gnats! In acquiring this vast and varied assortment of information, Pliny, in addition to his own extensive observations and experiences, read or had read to him, we are told, some two thousand volumes, many of which were by distinguished authors whose works have now completely perished.

On the arrangement and selection of his material, modern critics are almost unanimous in charging that the celebrated pantologist often reveals a glaring weakness in methodology and a serious lack of critical judgment; but notwithstanding these defects the *Natural History* is universally admitted to be a work which no student of things ancient can afford to ignore.

Remembering the far-flung fame of Ethiopia in the classical world, one well might expect that so catholic a student as Pliny undoubtedly was, manifested a considerable interest in the events and affairs of that ancient state. And, in truth, Pliny's Ethiopian notices are most numerous and illuminating; indeed, the *Natural History*, by actual account, contains more specific and distinct references to Ethiopia than are found in any other classical work. Some of these have to do with subjects and events recorded by the Greek writers already named, but in addition to these, there are scores of other most valuable matters which are mentioned in the extant works of no other ancient author.

Though Pliny is known to have visited Africa early in his life, the known facts about his itinerary there are very scarce; but there are no grounds whatever for supposing that he himself ever traveled in Ethiopia. His information seems to have been drawn altogether from the works of earlier writers, and happily he has preserved for us the names of many of these. A study of this list not only explains the source of the hitherto unrecorded facts which he mentions, but it sheds, incidentally, much light on the former existence of a number of ancient works treating the history of Ethiopia. Included in this list are, along with Herodotus, Eratosthenes, and Artemidorus, the names of five other authors of works on Ethiopia whom Pliny repeatedly cites as his authorities but who are otherwise unknown to students of ancient literature.

The earliest of these was a Greek named Dalion; his date is not definitely known, but he is supposed to have been a contemporary of Ptolemy II (Philadelphus) and hence must have flourished towards the end of the third century B.C. Dalion's writings seem to have been based to a considerable extent upon personal observation, for Pliny remarks that he "traveled a considerable distance beyond Meroe." Next was a Greek named Aristocreon, who appears to have lived at the close of the third or the beginning of the second century B.C. Pliny alludes to a work by this author in discussing the area of Ethiopia and the course of the Nile. Associated with Aristocreon is another writer named Basiles, who is said to have been the author of a treatise on Ethiopia. His exact date is not known, but Agatharchides mentioned him among the writers who had treated of the eastern portions of the world; hence he must have flourished earlier than the author. The best known writer in this group, and the one to whom Pliny most often referred, is an author named Bion. As nearly as may be determined, he too seems to have flourished in the second century B.C. Diogenes Laertius mentioned a man of this name who was the author of a book entitled *Ethiopica,* and Athenaeus records a citation which is thought to have been taken from this work. In commenting upon the passage in Acts 8:27, where the eunuch of Candace, queen of the Ethiopians, is recorded, Athanaeus makes the following remark: "The Ethiopians call every mother of the king Candace—they do not publish the [name of] fathers of the kings but hand them down as sons of the Sun. So says Bion in the first book of the Ethiopica." Although Atheneaus did not write until the third century A.D., there is hardly any doubt that the Bion here mentioned is the same as that referred to by Diogenenes Laertius and quoted by Pliny; thus it would seem that Bion's *Ethiopica* was fairly well known in the early centuries of the Christian era. From the notices taken from him by Pliny, it appears that Bion was well informed on the typographical details of the Nile Valley from Meroe northward to the boundaries of

Egypt, and the citation given by Athenaeus would seem to indicate that his work must have contained a valuable account of customs and manners of the Ethiopians. The last of the authors to be mentioned was a Greek, whom Pliny styled Simonides the Younger, and of whom it is said that he "made a stay of five years at Meroe when he wrote his account of Ethiopia." Aside from this reference, no other mention of this author or trace of his work has survived. Unfortunately, Pliny does not always indicate the particular source of the information he recorded concerning Ethiopia; hence it is difficult to tell to what extent he was specifically indebted to these several authors.

In addition to the aforementioned writers, notice may be taken of two other sources from which Pliny drew his information concerning Ethiopia. The first of these was a historical and geographical account of Africa composed in the latter part of the first century B.C. by Juba II, king first of Numidia and later Mauritania. On the death of his father, who was king of Numidia, in 46 B.C., Juba, while still a child, had been carried by Julius Caesar to Rome, where the young prince devoted himself to study with so much success that he soon became esteemed as one of the most learned men of his day. He subsequently married the daughter of Antony and Cleopatra, the princess who, as we have seen, was spirited away towards Ethiopia after the battle of Actium. Through his friendship with Augustus Caesar, Juba ultimately recovered his father's kingdom of Numidia which he later exchanged for the more extensive dominion of Mauritania.

From these connections with Africa, it is clear that much of Juba's knowledge must have been derived from personal observations or from informants who were personally acquainted with many of the matters which they transmitted to him. Judging from available remains of Juba's work, it appears that the greater part of it treated, as may be expected, the

northern or northwestern parts of the continent; that the
original treatise must have included an extensive sketch of
Ethiopia is indicated by the fact that there are in the *Natural
History* a number of detailed references to that distant king-
dom, which Pliny specifically credits to the work of the
Numidian king.

The last to be mentioned among Pliny's sources was
either a written or verbal report of the officers of an expedition dispatched to Ethiopia by the Emperor Nero a few years
before his death in 68 A.D. A sketch of the experiences and observations of the same expedition is recorded by the philosopher Seneca, the tutor and advisor of Nero, but the variations
in details of the report as given by Pliny and Seneca would
seem to indicate that Pliny did not draw his summary from
the account as recorded by the philosopher. Seneca specifically states that his notice is based on a verbal report
given him personally by two members of the expedition;
Pliny is less definite concerning his sources, but from the detailed character of his account, together with the fact that
much of his time was passed at the imperial court immediately
following the return of the expedition, it is quite likely that
his information was derived directly from one or more of the
explorers who had made the trip to Ethiopia.

With these remarks on what seem to have been Pliny's
principal sources, we may now examine the general character
of the information which he derived from these, and which
through his celebrated work he has transmitted to us. Emphasis will be placed, for the most part, on such notices as are not
found in the works of the authors already reviewed in this
survey.

According to Pliny the region designated in his day as
Ethiopia was in more ancient times known by different
names. The earliest of these was Aetherea, then Atlantia, and
third Aethiopia, which Pliny said was derived from Aethiops,

the son of Vulcan, the Latin name of the god of metalworking
and fire. Pliny does not specify the source of this tradition,
and so far as we are aware, it is not recorded by any other
classical writer.

Pliny's statement concerning the origin of the name Ethiopia is most interesting. Concerning the earlier history of
Ethiopia, Pliny wrote that it was "a famous and powerful
country as early as the time of the Trojan War when Memnon
was its king." He further observed that the legends connected
with Cephus and Andromeda, labeled members of the royal
house of Ethiopia, would seem to indicate that the kingdom
once "ruled over Syria and that its sway extended as far as the
shores of our [Mediterranean] Sea."

Of particular interest to the student of African history is a
series of lists enumerating the names of cities and towns lying
along the banks of the Nile, from the Egyptian border to Meroe. There are also lists giving the names of numerous cities
and towns and hitherto unnamed communities in the interior
of Ethiopia. These lists, taken in the main from the writings of
Bion, Juba, and Aristocreon, are among the most valuable
parts of Pliny's work, for although they are for the most part a
bare catalogue of names, they nevertheless constitute the
nearest approach to a gazetteer of ancient Ethiopia that is now
available to modern students. Moreover, they indicate that in
ancient times towns and cities were evidently very numerous
in Ethiopia. Pliny, quoting Bion, for example, gave the name
of forty-nine Ethiopian cities and towns between Syene and
Meroe; twenty-five of these were on the western side of the
Nile and twenty-four on the eastern side. Pliny cited Juba as
naming forty-one cities, towns, and communities located in
the same region. Some of those quotes from Bion are: on the
eastern side, south of Syene and north of Meroe, are Tacompsos, or Thatice, Aramasos, Sesamos, Sanduma, Masendomacam,
Arabeta, Boggia, Leupitorga, Tantarene, Mecinditae, Noa, Glo-

ploa, Gystate, Megada, Lea, Renni, Nups, Dorea, Patiga, Bacata, Dumuna, Rhadata, Boron, and Mallos; on the western side, Tacompsos, Maggore, Saea, Edos, Plenariae, Magassa, Buma, Linthuma, Spintum, Sydop, Pindicitora, Acug, Orsum, Sansa, Maumerum, Urbim, Molum, Pagoaraca, Zmanes, Mambli, Berressa, Acetuma, and "over against Meroe there was formerly a town called Epis which had however been destroyed before Bion wrote." In addition to the enumerations given by Bion and Juba, Pliny also named the following cities as those taken by the Roman general Petronius in the course of his invasion of Ethiopia in 24–23 B.C.: Pselcis Primis, Abuncis, Phthuris, Cambusis, Atteva, Stadasis, and Napata. Quoting Aristocreon, Pliny says there was on the western side of the Nile, and at a distance of five days' journey from Meroe, a city called Talles, and that twelve days' journey beyond Talles was another city known as Esar, which had been founded "by the Egyptians who deserted Psammetichus." Across the river from Esar was another town called Daron. He remarks, however, that the town which Aristocreon called Esar was designated by Bion as Sape. In the neighborhood of Esar, or Sape, was another city belonging to Egyptian deserters called Sembobitis, which was their capital. Eight days' journey farther south, but also situated on the Nile, was yet another town named Tenupis, which belonged to the Ethiopian Nubae. Scattered about in the same southern territory were still other towns, among them, according to Bion, Asara, Darde, Asel, Garodes, Navi, Mounda, Andatis, Secundum, Colligat, Secande, Navectabe, Cumi, Agrospi, Aegipa, Candrogari, Araba, and Summara.

Beyond these cities and towns, according to Pliny quoting Dalion, were a people called the Cisori, and another, the Nisyti, whose men are "remarkable for the unerring aim of their arrows." Farther along were still others known as the Longompori, the Oecalices, the Usibalci, the Isbeli, the Perusii, the Balii, and the Cespil; beyond these were regions inhabited

by the people of "fable only," according to Pliny quoting
Dalion.

The foregoing remarks by Pliny are valuable in that they
give us, in the first place, the names of scores of towns and
cities which would otherwise be totally unknown to history,
and, in the second place, these lists seem to indicate that
northern Ethiopia, today a sparsely inhabited, poverty-strick-
en, and rural district, was evidently an urbanized and pop-
ulous region in the centuries immediately preceding the
Christian Era. Shortly afterwards, this part of the country
seems to have been overtaken by some dire calamity, for Pliny
tells us that in his day most of the cities and towns given in
his lists were no longer in existence. Some years ago there was
a tendency on the part of scholars to distrust the full import of
Pliny's remarks in this respect, the prevailing opinion being
that no such array of cities and towns could ever have existed
in this now dreary and desolated area. Archeological explorations carried out in these parts during the past half-century or
so have, however, brought to light the buried ruins of scores
of ancient towns and cities which apparently date from the
very period to which Pliny and his authorities referred; indeed, several of the specific towns and cities named in the list
have been definitely located and identified to the complete
satisfaction of most critics. Notable among the discovery of
such ruins are those at Wad Ben Naga, which Sayce thought
might be identified with the ancient Talles of Pliny's list; the
ruins from the town of Saba, possibly the Sape or the Daron
of the ancients; and the ruins excavated by the Wellcome expedition at Gebel Moya. Here is yet another instance where
archeology has verified statements of the ancient writer.

Of the great city of Meroe, Pliny gave many interesting
and valuable particulars. Quoting as his authority the report
of the officers of the Meroe expedition, Pliny stated that "the
city of Meroe stands at a distance of seventy miles from the

first entrance of the Island of Meroe," south of the juncture of the Atbara and the Nile; that near the city "was a good harbor formed by an island named Tadu in the Nile"; that in the district in which the city stood, "the grass was of a greener and fresher color" than further north, and that there were "some slight appearances of forests"; that the city, although in a state of decay at the time of the visit of Nero's embassy, had formerly "enjoyed great renown and had maintained two hundred thousand soldiers and four thousand artisans"; that in the city there was "a great temple to Jupiter Amon, besides smaller shrines erected to his honor throughout all the country"; that the longest day at Meroe was twelve and a half hours, and that on "two days each year when the sun is in the 18th degree of Taurus and in the 14th of Leo it casts no shadows at noon in the city"; and that "the queens of the country bore the name Candace, a title that had passed from queen to queen for many years"; and finally, that "at the time of the visit of the Romans forty-five kings were said to have ruled over Ethiopia."

Modern research, supplemented by recent observations and excavations, have proved many of these statements to be true, or at the least in close conformity to historical fact. The location of Meroe as given by Pliny is approximately correct; the harbor formed by the island of Tadu is a fact; twice a year, on May 8 and August 4, no shadows are cast at noon in Meroe; the grass in the neighborhood of Meroe is "greener and of a fresher color" than farther north, and there are "some slight appearance of forests"; the ruins of the temple of Jupiter Amon were excavated by the Liverpool expedition in 1909–1910; remains of the "smaller shrines erected in his honor throughout all the country" have been located at several sites in the inland region of the Island of Meroe and elsewhere; archeological research by the same expedition has shown that about the first century A.D., the time of the visit of

Nero's expedition, the city of Meroe was evidently in a state
of decay, but that before it was a city of great and magnificent
buildings where "four thousand artisans" might well have
been employed to their fullest capacity.

In a similar manner, Pliny's statement that the name Candace "passed from queen to queen for many years" seems to
be confirmed by the recurring use of the term in connection
with many female members of the royal family by several ancient writers. Pseudo-Callisthenes, writing in the fourth century B.C., related that Alexander the Great paid a visit to "Candace," queen of Meroe; Strabo, in the first century B.C., used the
term in recording the clash between the Romans and the Ethiopians; Dion Cassius, a Roman historian of the second century
A.D., employed it in his version of the same event; and it occurs again in the eighth chapter of Acts in connection with
the story of Philip's conversion to Christianity of the Ethiopian official who had been on a visit to Jerusalem. For about
five hundred years, therefore, we find this title being employed by ancient writers as a designation for female members
of the royal family—a fact which strengthens considerably
Pliny's assertion that it was a practice of many years' standing.
It was formerly thought that these repeated references to
"Candace queen of the Ethiopians" indicated that the country
was anciently ruled by a line of queens, but Reisner, Griffith,
and other scholars now think that this was not the case; according to these authorities, the sovereignship of Ethiopia was
confined in the main to kings, and the title Candace referred
to queens or queen-mothers who doubtless ruled during the
minority of their sons. And Pliny's statement that forty-five
kings had ruled over Ethiopia before his time finds able testimony in the fact that Reisner has excavated the tombs and
recovered the names of more than two score Ethiopian sovereigns who reigned over the country for seven centuries before
the Christian era. Clearly, then, Pliny's works are a major
source for the reconstruction of ancient African history.

A valuable source of information about the world, including Africa, was written by Ptolemy, the renowned astronomer and geographer. He was a native of Egypt and wrote at Alexandria about the middle of the second century A.D. The system which he introduced by laying down places on the map according to their latitude and longitude is the one still in use today, and his map of the world was an enormous improvement over all those that preceded it: Very few places were accurately known from astronomical observations, however, and so Ptolemy applied the crudest means for ascertaining distance and direction, and obviously engaged in a good bit of guesswork. Still, his culminating work of ancient geography, written in Greek about 150 A.D., is of great value. By reason of his access to the stores of learning preserved in the great libraries of Alexandria, he was able to summarize in an orderly way the work of earlier scientific thinkers like Hipparchus, Eratosthenes, and Marinus of Tyre. His point of view was that of a mathematician, and his treatment was orderly and systematic for the time. His main work was devoted to astronomy and is contained in a book of significant influence on Arabic thought. It is still known by the name the Arabs gave it, *Almagest*.

Ptolemy's *Geography*, however, is not solely confined to the mathematical side of the subject but is also descriptive. For this work he collected much information from traders and travelers who came to Alexandria, then the greatest commercial center in the area. While his *Almagest* was fairly well known in the twelfth and thirteenth centuries through the Arabic version, his *Geography* was not so well known until after it was translated into Latin about 1410 A.D. After that time it began to exercise considerable influence on geographical thought.

Regarding Africa, it is not easy to gather from Ptolemy's study the precise limits of knowledge acquired by the ancients. On the eastern side of the continent the coast was reasonably familiar as far as Cape Guardafui, but it is also clear that enterprising merchants had occasionally made their way much farther south. Ptolemy mentions several who had sailed from Aromata (the Somali coast) past Cape Guardafui and on as far as Rhapta. This place has been identified as being located on the Tanganyika coast. He stated that from Rhapta southward to Cape Prasum, a gulf or shoaly sea extended, on the coast of which Ethiopians lived. These were probably the Bantu people, who for a long time were regarded as late comers to the East African coast, but who now are thought to have made an early appearance there. On the other hand, while Cape Prasum is conjectured to be today's Cape Delgado, Ptolemy's geography is not very accurate in this area.

In one regard, however, he made a wonderfully correct supposition. Based on information he received from traders returning from the interior, Ptolemy reported the existence of two large lakes and of mountains covered with snow; he at once concluded that the lakes must be the sources of the Nile and that the melting of the snow on the mountains was the cause of the periodic rise of that great river. In his map he placed the lakes very reasonably near their true position, and this gained credit among many modern writers for knowledge which later became important to explorers.

The final assessment of Ptolemy, however, is that he had no actual or firm information about any part of Africa distant from the coast and south of Cape Prasum, and this is confirmed by his showing the continent as making a sudden turn to the east just below his mountains of the Moon at the sources of the Nile, and extending in that direction until it joined Asia beyond the Malay peninsula, thus making the Indian Ocean, like the Mediterranean Sea, an inland body of water. For his time and centuries afterward, his work did inspire others who gradually reached the correct geographical limits of the world and Africa.

---

In sum, the great classical writers analyzed in this volume and their contributions to knowledge of Africa and African culture had a significant impact, both positive and negative, on European scholars, merchants, statesmen, explorers, missionaries, and colonialists for many centuries, reaching an apogee in the nineteenth century. One cannot really understand this continuity in history without reference to the classical writers—a continuity for which Hansberry has provided a useful synthesis and analysis. *Editor.*

# Bibliography

As pointed out in volume I of the *Notebook*, it is virtually impossible to list all of the sources Professor Hansberry examined during the course of his nearly fifty years of research in African studies. The reader is therefore informed that the list below contains only those works he specifically referred to in connection with classical writers and their views on Africa and Africans; the reader is further informed that Hansberry did not complete his bibliography before his death. The following is thus a partial bibliography.

The journals most frequently referred to in Hansberry's notes for this volume are: *Annals of Archaeology and Anthropology, Archaeological Review, Geography Journal, Journal of the East African Natural History Society, Kush, Sudan Notes and Records*. In addition, he examined articles on Kush and Ethiopia in the *Jewish Encyclopedia*.

The following is a list of more specific references, excluding those critically discussed in the several chapters.

Arkell, A. J. *Early Khartoum: An Account of the Excavation of an Early Occupation Site* . . . (London, 1949); *History of the Sudan* (London, 1961).

Baedeker, *Egypt* . . . (Leipzig, 1878–92), 2 vols.

Basset, Rene, "Berbers and North Africa," in James Hastings, ed., *Encyclopedia of Religion and Ethics* (New York, 1908–1922), 12 vols.

Beardsley, Grace H., *The Negro in Greek and Roman Civilization: A Study of the Ethiopian Type* (Baltimore and London, 1929).

Beazley, J. D., *Etruscan Vase-Painting* (Oxford, 1947); *Attic Black-Figure Vase Painters* (Oxford, 1956).

Berard, V., *Les Phéniciens et l'Odyssée* (Paris, 1902).

Boule, Marcellin, *Fossil Men: Elements of Human Palaeontology* . . . (Translated . . . with an Introduction by Jessie Elliot Ritchie and James Ritchie: Edinburgh, 1923).

Breasted, J. H., *Ancient Records of Egypt; Historical Documents from The Earliest Times to the Persian Conquest* . . . (Chicago, 1906–1907); 5 vols.

Browne, Henry, *Handbook of Homeric Study* (London, 1905).

Budge, E. A. W., *A History of Ethiopia, Nubia & Abyssinia* . . . (London, 1928), 2 vols.

————, *Annals of the Nubian Kings, With a Sketch of the History of the Nubian Kingdom of Napata* (London, 1912).

————, *The Egyptian Sudan; Its History and Monuments,* (London, 1907).

————, *Osiris: Studies on The History and Philosophy of Science, and on The History of Learning and Culture* (Bruges, 1936).

Bunbury, E. H., *A History of Ancient Geography Among The Greeks and Romans from The Earliest Ages Till The Fall of the Roman Empire* . . . (London, 1883), 2 vols.

Cailliaud, Frédéric, *Voyage à Meroe au fleuve Blanc, au-dela de Fazoql dans le Midi du royaume de Sennar, à Syouah et dans cinq autres oasis; fait dans les années 1819, 1820, 1821 et 1822* . . . (Paris 1826–27), 4 vols., and Atlas of 2 vols.

Cary, Max and E. H. Warmington, *The Ancient Explorers* (London, 1929).

Crowfoot, J. W., *The Island of Meroe* . . . *and Meroitic Inscriptions* (London, 1911).

Diodorus, Siculus, Book I.

Dunham, Dows, *Royal Cemeteries of Kush* (Boston, 1963).

Evans, A. J., "Egyptian Relations With Minoan Crete," *Journal of the Royal Archaeological Institute of Great Britain and Ireland* (London, 1898), vol. 55, pp. 215–223.

————, *The Palace of Minos: A Comparative Account of the Successive Stages of the Early Cretan Civilization as Illustrated by the Discoveries of Knossos . . .* (London, 1921–35), 4 vols.

————, *The Early Nilotic, Libyan and Egyptian Relations with Minoan Crete (London, 1925).*

Frost, K. T., "The Critias and Minoan Crete," *Journal of Hellenic Studies* (1913) vol. 33, p. 191.

Gardiner, A. H., *The Tomb of Huy, Viceroy of Nubia in the Reign of Tut'ankhamun . . .* (Copied in Lire and Colour by Nina de Garis Davies, and with Explanatory Text by Alan H. Gardiner . . . ; London, 1926).

Garstang, John, "Fifth Interim Report on the Excavations at Meroe," *Annals of Archaeology and Anthropology* (University of Liverpool, 1914), v. 7.

————, *Meroe, The City of the Ethiopians: Being an Account of a First Season's Excavations on the Site, 1909–1910 . . .* (Oxford, 1911).

————, *Guide to the 11th Exhibition: Excavation at Meroe* (Sudan Antiquities Service, 1912).

Griffith, F. L., "Meroitic Studies III and IV," *Journal of Egyptian Archaeology* (London, 1917), vol. 4, pp. 21–24, 159–173.

————, *Meroitic Inscriptions, Napata to Philae . . .* (London, 1912).

Hall, H. R. H., *The Ancient History of the Near East, from the Earliest Times to the Battle of Salamis . . .* (London, 1913).

Heeren, A. H. L. *Historical Researches into the Politics, Intercourse, and Trade of the Principal Nations of Antiquity . . .* (Translated from the German . . . ; Oxford, 1833–1834), 6 vols.

Hesiodus, *Hesiod, The Homeric Hymns, and Homerica* (with an English Translation . . . by H. G. Evelyn-White; London, 1914).

Hoskins, G. A., *Travels in Ethiopia, Above the Second Cataract of the Nile . . .* (London, 1835).

Jebb, R. C., *Greek Literature* (New York, 1890).

Johnston, H. H., *George Grenfell and the Congo; A History and Description of the Congo Independent State and Adjoining Districts of Congoland* . . . (London, 1908), 2 vols.

Knight, G. A. F., *Nile and Jordan: Being the Archaeological and Historical Interrelations Between Egypt and Canaan from the Earliest Times to the Fall of Jerusalem* . . . (London, 1921).

Lepsius, Karl Richard, *Denkmaeler aus Aegypten und Aethiopien nach den Zeichnungen der von Seiner Majestaet dem Koenige von Preussen Friedrich Wilhelm IV nach diesen Laendern gesendeten und in den Jahren 1842–1845 ausgefuehrten wissenschaftlichen Expedition* . . . (Berlin, 1849–56), 12 vols.

Littmann, Enno and Daniel Krencker, *Vorbericht der deutschen Aksum-expedition,* (Berlin, 1906).

Macmichael, H. A., *A History of the Arabs in the Sudan and Some Account of the People Who Preceded Them and of the Tribes Inhabiting Darfur* . . . (Cambridge, 1922), 2 vols.

MacKenzie, D. A., *Myths of Crete & Pre-Hellenic Europe* . . . (London, 1917).

Ministry of Finance, Survey Department, *The Archaeological Survey of Nubia, Report for 1907–1908* . . . (Cairo, 1910).

Naville, H. E., *The XIth Dynasty Temple of Deir el Behari,* (London, 1913), Part III.

Petrie, W. M. F., *A History of Egypt* . . . (London, 1898–1905), 6 vols.

———, *Syria and Egypt from the Tell el Amarna Letters* (n.p., 1898).

Pseudo-Callisthenes, *The History of Alexander the Great, Being the Syriac Version of the Pseudo-Callisthenes* . . . (Cambridge, 1889).

Publius Ovidius-Naso, *Metamorphoses,* Books IV, V.

Reisner, G. A., *Excavations at Kerma* . . . (Cambridge, Mass., 1923), vols. V, VI.

———, "The Meroitic Kingdom of Ethiopia," *Journal of Egyptian Archaeology* (Egypt Exploration Society, London, 1923), v. 9, pp. 34–77.

Seneca, L. A., *Naturales Quaestiones*, VI. 8.

Strabo, *Geography* (Literally Translated with Notes. The First 6 Books by H. C. Hamilton, the remainder by W. Falconer, London, 1889–1893), 3 vols.

Thomson, Arthur and D. R. MacIver, *The Ancient Races of the Thebaid: Being an Anthropometrical Study of the Inhabitants of Upper Egypt from the Earliest Prehistoric Times to the Moham-medan Conquest* . . . (Oxford, 1905).

Tozer, H. F., *A History of Ancient Geography* (Cambridge, 1935).

Woolley, C. L. and D. R. MacIver, *Karanog: The Romano-Nubian Cemetery* . . . (Philadelphia, 1910), 2 vols.

Yule, Henry, *Cathay and the Way Thither* (London, 1913–16), 4 vols.

Zupanic, N. M., "Les Premiers Habitants des Pays Yougo-slavs," *Revue Anthropologique* (Paris, 1919), p. 32.

# Index

# Africa and Africans As Seen by Classical Writers

*From the original Howard University Press edition, 1977.*

In this timely study, the eminent pioneer of African studies, William Leo Hansberry, examines classical references to the African continent and its people. The African designations in the writings of Homer, Hesiod, Ovid, Virgil, Herodotus, Pliny, Cassius, and others are discussed and analyzed in a lively, highly readable manner. Africa and Africans as Seen by Classical Writers reveals Hansberry's extensive knowledge of ancient Africa and confirms one of the author's major premises: that relations between blacks (Ethiopians) and Greeks of the post-Homeric age were more extensive than is usually noted by classical historians and scholars. It overwhelmingly affirms Africa's prominent role in the development of world civilization, a role which has but lately been too long ignored because of the denigratory legacy of colonialism and imperialism in the African continent.

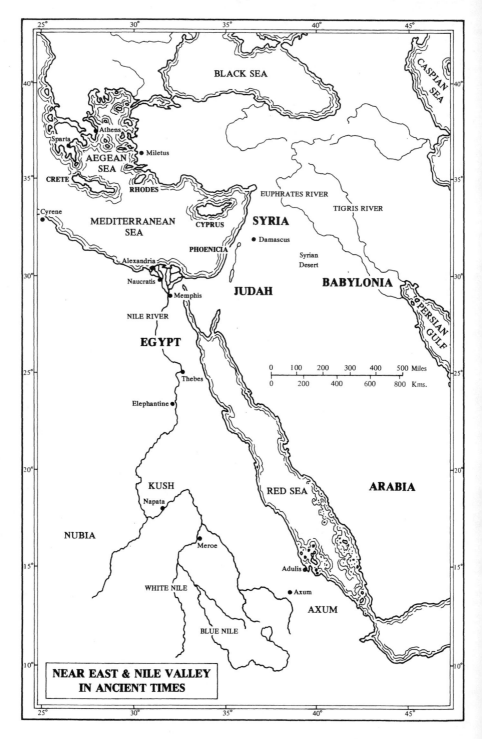

NEAR EAST & NILE VALLEY
IN ANCIENT TIMES